The
Jane
Austen
Treasury

The
Jane
Austen
Treasury

A delightful collection of
insights into her life, her times
and her novels

JANET TODD

ANDRE
DEUTSCH

THIS IS AN ANDRE DEUTSCH BOOK

This edition published in 2017

First published in 2013 as *Jane Austen: Her Life, Her Times, Her Novels*
by André Deutsch Limited
A division of the Carlton Publishing Group
20 Mortimer Street
London W1T 3JW

10 9 8 7 6 5 4 3 2

Text copyright © Janet Todd, 2013, 2017
Design © André Deutsch, 2017

Extracts from novels are taken from *The Cambridge Edition of the Works of
Jane Austen*, published by Cambridge University Press.
Extracts from letters are taken from *Jane Austen's Letters, Collected and Edited
by Deirdre Le Faye*, published by Oxford University Press.
All the images supplied in this publication are courtesy of Shutterstock.com

A catalogue record of this book is available from the British Library.

ISBN: 978 0 23300 514 0

Printed in Dubai

Contents

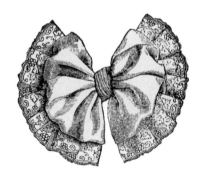

Introduction

Jane Austen is one of the greatest novelists in English literature. On the surface, her six published works appear simple romances; yet each is utterly distinct and each is complex in a different way. Her novels delight on first reading, but every further reading yields new and unexpected riches. As a result no individual reader ever exhausts her books, and each period sees something that speaks especially to its own concerns. The novels become new for every generation.

Austen is one of the rare literary figures who are loved alike by academic critics and by the general reading public. Through the last century and a half she has been subject to minute scholarly analysis of her plots and style, while through films and other adaptations her novels have become a global brand.

Like her works, Jane Austen herself has been subject of cult devotion. But, as with the novels, so with the author:

there are as many images as there are readers. Every new decade interprets her to fit its desires. In general in the late nineteenth century the prevailing image was created by her nephew, who depicted his aunt as a kindly and retiring spinster; the late twentieth century, however, stressed the professional woman writer who knew her own genius. Every reader has a private fantasy that she alone knows the real Jane Austen.

Jane Austen's universal popularity comes from many factors, but perhaps above all from her amazing ability to create believable and realistic characters living in a world that her first readers would have known, walking along country paths and urban streets we can still recognize today. Her subject is the relationship of people to their families and to the wider society, and she investigates a perennial dilemma: how a person can be true to herself and yet negotiate social pressures.

Jane Austen lived only forty-one years during the late eighteenth and early nineteenth centuries, but they were years of amazing turbulence and change. This colourful, transitional period stretched between two great revolutions: the French political one when she was still a child and the Industrial Revolution, which, as she grew into adulthood, was transforming Britain into the world's first urban industrial power. Jane Austen's subject (a few families in a country setting) seems largely to ignore both historical events in her novels. Yet in the detail and seemingly casual references there is much to be learned of both.

Through most of her life England was at war and her two naval brothers were in the thick of it. Military and naval personnel feature often in her novels. The war and the measures the British government had to take to keep the country united in support of its stance against revolutionary and later imperialistic France meant that authors had to be be cautious in what they wrote and be aware that even domestic descriptions might suggest wider social and political views.

In literary terms Jane Austen lived during the Romantic movement, the period of Wordsworth, Coleridge, Blake and Byron. Although in many ways she looks back to the literary style of her youth, especially to the poetical work of William Cowper whose subject is the rural life she also made hers, in her later novels she was in tune with Romantic sensibility in her depiction of changed psychological states and in her emotional use of scenery. Often, however, the ironic attitude that marked so much of her writing touched her descriptions of young women losing themselves in an enthusiasm for natural beauty.

Jane Austen lived just before photography made the world seem black and white; she has become synonymous with the colour, fantasy and romance of the Regency period which she so brilliantly portrayed.

1

Early Life

Jane Austen is not an overtly autobiographical writer: she describes no lady author or witty spinster in her novels and no heroine rejects marriage as she did or cruelly mocks a neighbour with impunity.

The story of her life comes instead from her letters, mainly written to her beloved sister Cassandra (who, however, destroyed the majority before she died in 1845), and from pious memoirs by her clergyman brother Henry and Victorian nephew James Edward Austen Leigh. She herself left no diary, and her correspondence begins only in 1796 when she was already twenty; several periods are uncovered by letters.

So a lot of her life remains secret, a fact which has inspired much invention by later admirers, much fantasizing about clandestine lovers and sexual proclivities

– and about the "real" woman. There are as many Jane Austens as there are readers: the nineteenth century on the whole desired a kindly and retiring lady, the twentieth a repressed romantic heroine, and the twenty-first a professional author and psychotherapist.

Jane Austen was born on 16 December 1775 into a family network that stretched from rich landowners through clerics down to an apprentice milliner and included an alleged shoplifter and a bankrupt banker. George Austen, her father, was a cultivated rector in the small village of Steventon in the southern English county of Hampshire; her mother, Cassandra, daughter of a former fellow of Oxford's All Souls College, had aristocratic connections. In time George would amass a library of over five hundred books and, according to his son Henry, was "a profound scholar" with "most exquisite taste"; his wife composed witty verses for pupils and friends.

As was usual at the time, George Austen obtained a living through patronage, with the help of the wealthy Thomas Knight, husband of a second cousin. An uncle provided another parish, and Knight, who owned much land around Steventon, rented him a farm, which added about a third to his income. But the earnings never quite kept pace with the growing family and George also prepared a few paying pupils for university: these shared the rectory with his own children. All in all, the Austens were reasonably placed socially and financially, on the edge of the gentry rather than securely within their ranks. The nuances, concerns and anxieties of this middling class would become Jane Austen's especial subject. She would sometimes lovingly display them, but more often expose their limitations, their prejudices and self-deceptions – especially when privileged by gender, birth or function: husband, clergyman, soldier or landowner.

George and Cassandra had eight children. Wet nursing was common in families of their rank and after a few weeks or months the babies would be sent from home to be fed and kept for a year or two. Jane would live with her mother all her life but there is little evidence of closeness; perhaps this common practice contributed to some distance.

Of the boys, one was disabled and sent away to live elsewhere, being hardly mentioned in family records; the others did reasonably well through patronage or effort. James followed his father into the Steventon living; his family would be left a considerable fortune through his mother's relations, the Leighs. Edward was adopted as a child by the rich Knight relatives, in due course changed his name to Knight, and inherited Godmersham Park, Chawton Manor and Steventon.

When not even twelve years old Frank and Charles entered the naval academy, rising through the ranks during the wars with France from 1793 to 1815: through sheer longevity (ninety-one and seventy-three respectively) they became admirals. Henry joined the militia, then became a prosperous banker and army agent, but fell on hard times in March 1816 after the war finally ended; he then entered the Church.

The contrast between the boys and the two Austen girls is stark. In 1792 the feminist writer Mary Wollstonecraft pleaded for equal education and entry into some professions for girls. Such radical theories did not impress many, and Jane and her older sister Cassandra had no obvious opportunity to gain a good income. Only marriage would promise independence from the family; if they remained unmarried, they would be required to be generally useful as companions and occasional nurses. During her father's lifetime, Jane received £20 a year for spending on charity and herself.

Austen commented obliquely on women's total dependency on men when in her letters she lamented their inability to travel except with male assistance, and she allows the genteel but poor Jane Fairfax in *Emma* to compare (with pardonable exaggeration) being a governess to being a slave or prostitute. The anxiety of a future without marriage or income shadows all her fictional women without fortunes. In her letters, however, there is an equal fear of what marriage might mean for the fertile woman (which so many of the Austen wives seemed to be), the relentless round of childbearing; she wrote of her much-loved and once-more-pregnant niece Anna: "Poor Animal, she will be worn out before she is thirty.—I am very sorry for her."

Jane and Cassandra were not without formal education. In the Easter of 1783 they were dispatched to Oxford to be tutored by Mrs Cawley; they returned in the autumn following an outbreak of typhus – from which Jane herself nearly died. Then for two years they attended the Abbey House School, Reading, with Mrs La Tournelle, famed for her cork leg and theatrical manner. Perhaps the fees were a drain on the Austen household for by the close of 1786 the sisters were back in Steventon. From then on they picked up an education in the family – and probably a good deal from each other, for they were always extremely close. Jane valued a well-stocked mind but never set much store by formal education – for boys or girls. Native wit and commonsense, together with firm morality and an aptitude for thoughtfulness and reading, would always overtop intellectual research and training through public school and university.

As a child she parodied the dull histories that were written to educate children, especially Oliver Goldsmith's *History of England from the Earliest Times to the Death of George II*. The family's copy includes Jane's furiously partisan marginal comments, lauding the Stuarts, the originally Scottish royal house which included the ill-fated Mary, Queen of Scots and the executed Charles I, and came to an end with the deposing of James II. She lambasted their enemies as "impudent", "detestable" and part of a "Bad Breed". Enthusiastically she comments "Spoken like a Tory", and, responding to praise of the detested Elizabeth I, she exclaims, "A Lie – an entire lie from beginning to end". It was as well that she wrote her own history – with illustrations by her sister.

2

Early Writings

J ane Austen was a precocious, alarmingly assured child. From the age of eleven she was looking at the adult world with wide, clear eyes, amused at the emotions, deceptions, reading habits, intrigues and bustle of family and friends.

As proof, she left twenty-two little stories and plays with titles such as "The Adventures of Mr Harley", "The Beautiful Cassandra", "The Generous Curate" and "The Mystery". Some are just a few lines long, but all are carefully written out in three notebooks which she kept by her all her life.

The majority of the pieces created before she was fifteen are comical, ebullient, anarchic and often surreal. They treat self-indulgence and wickedness of all sorts: gluttony, drunkenness, matricide, theft and total self-absorption, all embodied in cheery characters without a shred of shame.

Very unusually for a child so young, the earliest pieces mock grown-up fiction. Jane was born into a family of readers: they read poetry, sermons, history and, above all, novels. Serious works were purchased by her clergyman father; trivial fiction was borrowed from the circulating library.

"Frederic and Elfrida", written when Jane was eleven or twelve, parodies the standard romances of the 1780s. It's full of overblown emotion and improbable behaviour: Frederic and Elfrida "loved with mutual sincerity, but were both determined not to transgress the rules of Propriety by owning their attachment, either to the object beloved, or to any one else". Adult manners and unmeaning compliments show up the disparity between what's said and thought: here when the heroine encounters a new friend she exclaims, "Lovely & too charming Fair one, notwithstanding your forbidding Squint, your greasy tresses & your swelling Back, which are more frightfull than imagination can paint or pen describe, I cannot refrain from expressing my raptures, at the engaging Qualities of your Mind, which so amply atone for the Horror with which your first appearance must ever inspire the unwary visitor." The commonsensical and ordinary only occasionally irrupt into the story: after nearly twenty years of delicate romantic waiting, Elfrida, sensing a youthful rival, tells Frederic she'll marry him at once – at which he "boldly replied: 'Damme, Elfrida, you may be married tomorrow but I won't.'" Happily, Elfrida's repeated fainting fits bring him to heel.

The amoral and headstrong female rogue, a regular feature of Jane's early tales, first appears as Eliza in "Henry and Eliza". At three months this amazing child can give her putative parents "sprightly answers"; at eighteen she's caught stealing a £50 banknote and turned out of doors, "happy in the conscious knowledge of her own Excellence". In an adventurous life she avoids being "put to Death in some torturelike manner" but not having her fingers eaten by her ravenous children – whom she'd forgotten to feed. She ends her amoral career with "the Blessings of thousands, & the Applause of her own Heart". Eliza has energy and resourcefulness: she uses everything to hand, whether her fine clothes or a rope ladder, singing, living high, begging, walking vast distances, all with the same verve with which she gets through £18,000 a year when married, an enormous sum almost twice what Mr Darcy will receive in *Pride and Prejudice*.

The jaunty rogue appears again in the most extended of the youthful parodies, "Love & Freindship" (Austen's spelling), written in 1790 when Jane was fourteen. The heroine Laura, now fifty-five and presumed by others (but not herself) to be safe from the advances of "disagreeable Lovers", tells the story of a life full of sentimental attitudes, the staple of popular fiction. For example, a Noble Youth whom Laura and her family meet in the romantic vale of Usk tells them how he refused to marry the woman his father chose for him: "'Never shall it be said that I obliged my Father.' We all admired the noble Manliness of his reply." When the father asked, "Where, Edward, in the name of wonder […] did you pick up this unmeaning gibberish? You have been studying Novels I suspect", the Noble Youth "scorned to answer".

Unlike the earlier tales, "Love & Freindship" includes some sensible characters who comment both on the craziness of romantic behaviour and on the absurdity of much escapist fiction. Here is the beginning of the sort of character Austen will later be famous for creating, one to whom readers can relate within the story.

Jane Austen's first three published novels were drafted soon after these tales were written and, in the early versions, may well have had much in common with them. The cliché of love at first sight, so silly in the tales, becomes a damaging belief in *Sense and Sensibility* and influences the title of an early version of *Pride and Prejudice*, "First Impressions". The topsy-turvy morality of Laura or Eliza or the Noble Youth, which justifies any act on the basis that it feels good to the actor, will be more seriously treated in the misguided Marianne and self-seeking Lucy Steele.

To the end of her life Jane Austen will laugh at the sentimental and naively didactic fiction of her contemporaries, both at the improbability of the characters and plots and at the tendency to end with resounding morals. The message given by the appallingly selfish Laura in "Love & Freindship", just before she dies of pneumonia from a fainting fit on the damp ground, is "Run mad as often as you chuse; but do not faint—". At the end of *Northanger Abbey* the narrator tells her reader: "I leave it to be settled by whomsoever it may concern, whether the tendency of this work be altogether to recommend parental tyranny, or reward filial disobedience."

Although there are continuities, Jane Austen left much behind when she grew up and into print. The six finished novels will lack the exuberance of the juvenile works: the Rabelaisian treatment of pregnancy, drunkenness, gluttony, cannibalism, age and death. But she always kept the impulse of the child, and her niece Anna recalls that "she would tell us the most delightful stories chiefly of Fairyland, and her Fairies had all characters of their own—".

In these childhood tales Jane Austen comes through loud and clear: a clever, literary child in a large clever family, a girl among educated brothers who must entertain to be noticed. Her mingling of clear sight, desire to tease and appetite for absurdity promises the later brilliant ironist.

THE BEAUTIFUL CASSANDRA

CHAPTER THE FIRST

CASSANDRA was the Daughter & the only
Daughter of a celebrated Millener in Bond Street.
Her father was of noble Birth, being the near relation
of the Dutchess of —'s Butler.

CHAPTER THE 2D

WHEN Cassandra had attained her 16th year, she
was lovely & amiable, & chancing to fall in love with
an elegant Bonnet her Mother had just compleated,
bespoke by the Countess of —, she placed it on her
gentle Head & walked from her Mother's shop to
make her Fortune.

CHAPTER THE 3D

THE first person she met, was the Viscount
of —, a young Man, no less celebrated for his
Accomplishments & Virtues, than for his Elegance &
Beauty. She curtseyed & walked on.

CHAPTER THE 4TH

SHE then proceeded to a Pastry-cook's, where she
devoured six ices, refused to pay for them, knocked
down the Pastry Cook & walked away.

Chapter the 5th

SHE next ascended a Hackney Coach & ordered it to Hampstead, where she was no sooner arrived than she ordered the Coachman to turn round & drive her back again.

Chapter the 6th

BEING returned to the same spot of the same Street she had set out from, the Coachman demanded his Pay.

Chapter the 7th

SHE searched her pockets over again & again; but every search was unsuccessfull. No money could she find. The man grew peremptory. She placed her bonnet on his head & ran away.

Chapter the 8th

THRO' many a street she then proceeded & met in none the least Adventure, till on turning a Corner of Bloomsbury Square, she met Maria.

Chapter the 9th

CASSANDRA started & Maria seemed surprised; they trembled, blushed, turned pale & passed each other in a mutual silence.

CHAPTER THE 10TH

CASSANDRA was next accosted by her freind the Widow, who squeezing out her little Head thro' her less window, asked her how she did? Cassandra curtseyed & went on.

CHAPTER THE 11th

A QUARTER of a mile brought her to her paternal roof in Bond Street, from which she had now been absent nearly 7 hours.

CHAPTER THE 12th

SHE entered it & was pressed to her Mother's bosom by that worthy Woman. Cassandra smiled & whispered to herself "This is a day well spent."

3

"Lady Susan"

The most flamboyant figure in Jane's childhood was her cousin Eliza, fourteen years her senior, to whom she dedicated her longest childhood work, "Love & Freindship". Eliza was the daughter of George Austen's sister Philadelphia, who went to India to marry the physician Tysoe Saul Hancock.

They had one daughter, rumoured to be the result of Philadelphia's affair with Warren Hastings, the future Governor-General of British India (Hastings provided a £10,000 trust fund for the child).

In 1781 Eliza married an aristocratic French captain in the dragoons and became Countess de Feuillide. In February 1794, during the Terror that followed the French Revolution and while Eliza and her son were in England, de Feuillide was guillotined. Their one son, the sickly Hastings, died in 1801.

A lively, sociable woman, Eliza stayed in the Steventon parsonage with the Austens for lengthy periods, flirting with Jane's brothers: the eldest and most literary James and the more dashing and military Henry. In 1797 she married Henry – while continuing to flirt: she declared she had "an aversion to the word husband and never ma[d]e use of it". By some accounts, after James himself married, his new wife feared her husband retained his admiration for the fascinating cousin.

When staying in Steventon, Eliza threw herself into the theatricals which so delighted the Austen children. The young seem to have preferred the comic and satirical, such as Sheridan's *The Rivals*, to the tragic and sentimental, like Thomas Francklin's *Matilda*, but plays of all sorts were read and acted, sometimes elaborately in the rectory barn. In Susannah Centlivre's *The Wonder! A Woman Keeps a Secret* Eliza de Feuillide played the flirtatious leading lady and "all the young folks" took part.

The glamorous Eliza (described by a friend as a "pretty wicked looking Girl with bright Black Eyes") must have thoroughly impressed her young cousin, and Jane's depiction of sparkling but not quite proper women, from the delightful Elizabeth Bennet, first created in the 1790s, to the amoral Mary Crawford of *Mansfield Park* (1814), may have been nurtured by this exciting lady.

Long before *Mansfield Park*, Eliza may be discerned in the remarkable novella Jane wrote probably in 1794–5, about the time when her cousin was fascinating both James and Henry. "Lady Susan" is a romantic black comedy written in letters. An accomplished work, it is far more realistic than any of the juvenile tales but quite distinct from the published novels in style and content. It tells of an unscrupulous, predatory and beautiful widow with a shy virtuous daughter, Frederica, who thoroughly irritates her sophisticated mother. Lady Susan has an affair with a friend's husband, then sets out to win his daughter's stupid but rich suitor Sir James for Frederica; after that, she seduces her sister-in-law's virtuous but priggish brother Reginald de Courcy. She is unmasked only when she fails to keep her various lovers apart; she ends up consoling herself for the failure by marrying the foolish Sir James herself and leaving the virtuous De Courcy for her insipid daughter.

Lady Susan is villainous, but her energy is beguiling. She manoeuvres in a world politically and financially controlled by men, her only tools being her wit and beauty. She knows the power of these: "Consideration and Esteem as surely follow command of Language, as Admiration waits on Beauty," she writes to an approving friend. Although her various schemes in the end do not answer, like the jaunty heroines of Jane's juvenile works she remains undismayed and undaunted and, quite unlike in most of the didactic stories written by women of the time, this rakish heroine has no desire to repent and reform on the last page.

When "Lady Susan" was finally published in 1871 it was regarded as indecorous and, "thoroughly unpleasant in its characters and its detail" (*The Nation*). Later critics rather enjoyed the heroine's spiritedness and mastery of language, even discerning a likeness between her eloquence and Jane Austen's own artistry.

4

Northanger Abbey

From about 1795 Jane Austen was sketching out three full-length novels clearly intended for more than family amusement: "Elinor and Marianne", which would become *Sense and Sensibility*; "First Impressions", an early version of *Pride and Prejudice*; and "Susan", forerunner of *Northanger Abbey*.

In 1797 her proud father had offered to send one of the first two to the prestige publisher Thomas Cadell – who declined the offer "by Return of Post". "Susan", drafted probably in 1798–9, was, it seems, closest in tone to the early comic tales and is the first work Jane Austen herself sent – and sold – to a publisher: in spring 1803 Benjamin Crosby, a trade publisher serving circulating libraries, paid £10 for the manuscript. Curiously he never published it: perhaps on reflection he didn't care for the way it seemed to poke fun at gothic fiction, a genre in which he himself had a financial interest.

Proclaimed a dull ordinary girl by the narrator, Catherine, the heroine of *Northanger Abbey*, is raised by principled, unimaginative parents. To her mother her daughter appears a "sad little shatter-brained creature", inept both at housekeeping and at memorizing historical facts. She is taken by the local landowner and his trivial, clothes-obsessed wife from her village to fashionable Bath, where she is introduced both to the popular gothic fiction her parents never read and to the habitual liars she hasn't encountered in her sheltered life. Initially she believes both to be true.

Austen's novel is the portrait of a naive reader learning the value and limits of fiction. Catherine's novel-reading leads her into many blunders, especially when she's invited to what she assumes will be a gothic abbey – though it's in fact a thoroughly modernized mansion. But in the process of the novel she learns to scrutinize her own reactions and trust to probability; she learns that language is not always used simply to represent reality and that novels are not real life, but that, read carefully and intelligently, they could help a reader judge and interpret real life. *Northanger Abbey* is also a romantic story of a pleasant young girl managing to attract a clever hero through her teachability and obvious adoration of himself. Henry Tilney is an attractive man to read about, but possibly rather difficult to live with considering the way he echoes his dominating father (when his father is absent) and his tendency to enjoy his

MUSLIN

Indian chintz and muslins (from Dacca or Bengal) were an important part of East India Company trade from the mid-1600s. The cheap, pretty, brightly coloured fabrics were so popular in England in the early 1700s that they influenced the British woollen and silk trades. UK manufacture of muslin started in Scotland in 1779 with the invention of the spinning mule by Samuel Crompton. Soon British muslins flooded the market, supported by sharp increases in import duties for Indian fabrics. By 1793 a report by the directors of the East India Company stated that "every shop offers British muslins for sale equal in appearance and of more elegant patterns than those of India, for one-fourth, or, perhaps, more than one-third less in price". Initially British manufacturers could not match the dyeing skill of Indian suppliers, so most British muslins were white or unbleached. Coloured and patterned (particularly spotted) muslins continued to be popular and therefore imported.

own superiority. But all will be well as long as Catherine remains impressionable.

The book that so entrances Catherine is Ann Radcliffe's *The Mysteries of Udolpho* (1794), one of the best and most influential gothic novels written during the craze for such fiction in the 1790s and early 1800s. Taken en masse, this fiction presents a frightening picture of Catholic Europe during the long English war against France. In these often formulaic and repetitive stories, sensational melodramatic events take place in exotic landscapes of high mountains with mysterious castles and monasteries peopled by brigands, devilish monks and would-be rapists. The usually orphaned, temperamentally rather English heroines face commanding, threatening villains, who yet have a certain charisma to which the heroine is not always immune. Perhaps because they sensed the sexual undertones, moralists inveighed against sensational novels which, through circulating libraries, were now within the reach of middle-class girls and their servants. They feared that promiscuous reading would ruin young women for ordinary real-life marriage. They could also have feared that some of the extreme situations of male power depicted in gothic fiction, shorn of exotic locations and habits, might seem a little close to what a girl could face in contemporary British life.

Jane Austen burlesques the effect of Radcliffe on a susceptible girl, but she also knows the joy of reading such carefully crafted works and she is not in the business of denigrating her sister authors: "I will not

THE PICTURESQUE

The picturesque was a craze in the late eighteenth century when tourism within England became fashionable for the middle classes. Its main theorist was the artist and educationalist William Gilpin (1724–1807): Henry Austen wrote that "at a very early age" his sister was "enamoured of Gilpin on the Picturesque". In essence, the picturesque was "that kind of beauty which would look well in a picture", a way of seeing the natural through the cultural. In *Northanger Abbey* Tilney and his sister, standing with Catherine on Bath's Beechen Cliff, instruct her to compose a scene by noting foreground, middle distance and background, and by seeing texture, light and shade, all to create an aesthetic whole.

The picturesque movement was especially associated with the landscape gardening of "Capability" Brown and his successor Humphrey Repton, who transformed the grounds of English estates from regular patterns into "natural" landscapes of artificial lakes, irregular groups of trees and wide lawns (sometimes shifting whole villages in the process).

Northanger Abbey is not entirely respectful of the movement: absurdly Catherine learns to reject the view of Bath and, more importantly, General Tilney suggests moving a cottage simply to enhance a view.

adopt that ungenerous and impolitic custom so common wih novel writers, of degrading by their contemptuous censure the very performances, to the number of which they are themselves adding—." The boorish man fails to appreciate *Udolpho*, while the hero understands its power: Catherine is not entirely mocked when she says, "while I have Udolpho to read, I feel as if nobody could make me miserable". Austen's own ability to make her readers keep turning her pages suggests she learnt much from this sort of popular fiction.

Although the novels the heroine is actually urged to read are gothic and "horrid", the writers who are praised directly by the narrator are more realistic authors, aspects of whose art Jane Austen very much admired: Maria Edgeworth and Fanny Burney. *Evelina*, published in 1778 by a youthful Burney, sets the pattern for Austen's own novel in its portrayal of a virtuous but naive girl entering society and, while falling in love, learning how to comport herself in the fashionable world.

Northanger Abbey was published posthumously in 1818. Shortly before she died Austen had been preparing the novel for publication, revising it but not changing its identity. It remained a novel of her youth, expressing the 1790s. She was always attuned to the detail of "period, places, manners, books, and opinions", as she put it in her Advertisement, whether a matter of bonnets and muslins (a topic of much concern in the novel) or of cultural crazes like the "picturesque" and the gothic. Possibly, had she lived, she'd have gone on tinkering with the novel to make it more contemporary or more clearly historical, since her last words on it from a letter dated March 1817 are: "Miss Catherine is put upon the Shelve for the present, and I do not know that she will ever come out."

EXTRACT FROM *NORTHANGER ABBEY*

*The heroine, Catherine Morland, has just been introduced
to gothic fiction by her new friend Isabella Thorpe. She
is enthralled by Radcliffe's suspenseful* Mysteries of
Udolpho *– which reveals its secrets only at the end.
Radcliffe had many less skilful imitators and Catherine is
eager to read their "horrid" works as well.*

[Isabella to Catherine] "Have you gone on with
Udolpho?"

"Yes, I have been reading it ever since I woke; and I
am got to the black veil."

"Are you, indeed? How delightful! Oh! I would not
tell you what is behind the black veil for the world!
Are not you wild to know?"

"Oh! Yes, quite; what can it be? But do not tell
me — I would not be told upon any account. I know
it must be a skeleton, I am sure it is Laurentina's
skeleton. Oh! I am delighted with the book! I should
like to spend my whole life in reading it. I assure
you, if it had not been to meet you, I would not have
come away from it for all the world."

"Dear creature! How much I am obliged to you;
and when you have finished Udolpho, we will read

the Italian together; and I have made out a list of ten or twelve more of the same kind for you."

"Have you, indeed! How glad I am! — What are they all?"

"I will read you their names directly; here they are, in my pocketbook. Castle of Wolfenbach, Clermont, Mysterious Warnings, Necromancer of the Black Forest, Midnight Bell, Orphan of the Rhine, and Horrid Mysteries. Those will last us some time."

"Yes, pretty well; but are they all horrid, are you sure they are all horrid?"

5

Loves

Jane enjoyed flirtations. The one most appealing to posterity was with the shy, attractive Thomas Lefroy from Ireland, who was studying to be a barrister. During part of 1795–6 he stayed with relatives at a neighbouring rectory – and danced with Jane at three local balls. Excitedly she wrote to Cassandra, "Imagine to yourself everything most profligate and shocking in dancing and sitting down together."

But no marriage proposal came from the young man, whose family certainly expected him to marry for more money than the younger daughter of a country clergyman could deliver; Jane soon reported to her sister, "I am to flirt my last with Tom Lefroy, & when you receive this it will all be over." Tom went on to become Lord Chief Justice of Ireland. He later told a nephew that he had had a "boyish love" for Jane Austen.

EXTRACT FROM *SENSE AND SENSIBILITY*

[Marianne]"Mama, you are not doing me justice.
I know very well that Colonel Brandon is not old
enough to make his friends yet apprehensive of
losing him in the course of nature. He may live
twenty years longer. But thirty-five has nothing to
do with matrimony."

"Perhaps," said Elinor, "thirty-five and seventeen
had better not have anything to do with matrimony
together. But if there should by any chance happen
to be a woman who is single at seven and twenty, I
should not think Colonel Brandon's being thirty-five
any objection to his marrying *her*."

"A woman of seven and twenty," said Marianne,
after pausing a moment, "can never hope to feel
or inspire affection again, and if her home be
uncomfortable, or her fortune small, I can suppose
that she might bring herself to submit to the offices
of a nurse, for the sake of the provision and security
of a wife. In his marrying such a woman, therefore
there would be nothing unsuitable. It would be a
compact of convenience, and the world would be
satisfied. In my eyes it would be no marriage at all,
but that would be nothing. To me it would seem only
a commercial exchange, in which each wished to be
benefited at the expense of the other."

> "It would be impossible, I know," replied Elinor, "to convince you that a woman of seven and twenty could feel for a man of thirty-five anything near enough to love to make him a desirable companion to her. [...]"

Cassandra Austen's romantic hopes were early blighted. Since childhood she had known her father's pupil Tom Fowle. He had become a clergyman with an income too small to support a wife; so when Cassandra accepted his marriage proposal in 1792 they anticipated a long engagement. Apparently unaware of this engagement, Lord Craven, Tom Fowle's patron, asked his protégé to travel with him as his chaplain to the West Indies. They set off in early 1796; in February of the following year, just as the Steventon family were expecting his return, they received news that he had died of yellow fever off St Domingo and had been buried at sea. He left his savings of £1,000 to Cassandra; it would always provide a small income for her. She remained unmarried for the rest of her life.

Jane's youth came to an abrupt end in 1801 when her father decided to make his son James curate of Steventon, sell his farming lease and move to Bath, where he could live on the tithe income from his parishes. In Bath, the most celebrated spa town in England, his wife could take the waters for her health and they could all benefit from the entertainments of a fashionable town with assembly rooms and gardens. The two daughters Cassandra and Jane would accompany them.

Her parents' decision to move from the country was perhaps a shock to Jane, who is reputed to have fainted when she heard of it. But her letters suggest ambivalence at leaving her first home. In January 1801, she wrote: "there is something interesting in the bustle of going away, & the prospect of spending future summers by the Sea or in Wales is very delightful [...] It must not be generally known however that I am not sacrificing a great deal in quitting the Country – or I can expect to inspire no tenderness, no interest in those we leave behind."

The Austens rented rooms in Sydney Place; three years later they moved to Green Park Buildings East. There is so little information concerning Jane's five years in Bath that speculation has burgeoned. Was she too unhappy to do much writing? Was she simply more busy and bustling than she had been in the country? Did she fall in love passionately, hopelessly, sadly, or not at all?

One event has emerged from the obscurity through her niece Caroline's (second-hand) recollections. When nearly twenty-seven, the age at which her fictional characters fear that the chance of love is over, she made one of several visits back to Hampshire. There she stayed with her old friends, the landed Bigg family in Manydown near Steventon. Harris Bigg-Wither, a tall, plain, rather awkward and stuttering young man, was heir to the estate; one evening he proposed marriage to Jane and she accepted him. Six years her junior, he was not a romantic prospect, but her fondness for his sisters and the offer of an independent life as mistress of a great house instead of dependence in lodgings in Bath must have been attractive. However she quickly had a "revulsion of feeling", perhaps after consulting Cassandra. Next morning she informed Harris she had changed her mind. The sisters left Manydown at once. Two years later Harris married; he would father ten children. Jane continued her friendship with his sisters.

Other visits were less dramatic – and also more hidden. She stayed at the great house of Godmersham in Kent where her brother Edward lived with his growing family – seven children by 1802. With various family members she took holidays on the Devon coast, probably in Sidmouth, in Wales by the sea, and later at Lyme Regis in Dorset, which would provide a setting within her final completed novel *Persuasion*. Cassandra's watercolour sketch of Jane from behind was made on a walk near Lyme. (If only she had turned around!)

Family tradition has it that on one of the seaside visits she met a man she truly loved but that he died shortly after. Whatever Jane Austen's main reasons for not marrying, her love of writing must have played some part in her decision. As she wrote to her niece Fanny Knight just before her death in 1817, "what a loss it will be, when you are married. You are too agreeable in your single state... I shall hate you when your delicious play of Mind is all settled down into conjugal & maternal affections."

EXTRACT FROM *PERSUASION*

[Anne Elliot to Captain Harville] "... I should deserve utter contempt if I dared to suppose that true attachment and constancy were known only by woman. No, I believe you capable of every thing great and good in your married lives. I believe you equal to every important exertion, and to every domestic forbearance, so long as — if I may be allowed the expression, so long as you have an object. I mean, while the woman you love lives, and lives for you. All the privilege I claim for my own sex (it is not a very enviable one, you need not covet it) is that of loving longest, when existence or when hope is gone."

6

"The Watsons"

By the time she moved from Steventon to Bath, Jane Austen had three novels in manuscript and several works not intended for the public eye, such as "Lady Susan" and "Love & Freindship". In about 1804 she began writing a novel rather different from anything she'd tried before, a harsher, more claustrophobic work realistically depicting the difficulties facing unmarried daughters with no fortune.

She wrote forty pages of "The Watsons", making many corrections and inserting revisions on new bits of paper. She obviously changed her mind about details as she went along, suggesting that the fictional world was not quite clear in her mind. There are no complete manuscripts of Jane Austen's novels and only fair copies of the juvenile writings, so this work is extremely valuable for critics interested in her method of composition.

"The Watsons" describes an ailing clergyman on a small income with four unmarried daughters. There's none of the jollity in this family of girls that characterizes the Bennets of *Pride and Prejudice*; instead there's anxiety and cruel rivalry. The heroine, Emma, has been taken from her home by a wealthy widowed aunt and brought up genteelly; her expectations are dashed when the aunt marries a fortune-hunter. She returns home better educated and more refined than her sisters but with no greater fortune. Two of the sisters are desperately seeking husbands and are prepared to wreck each other's chances in the struggle. The eldest, the kindly Elizabeth, claims she could be content unmarried if she had any income but that "it is bad to grow old and be poor and laughed at". She knows more than Emma of life in the lower ranks: when Emma claims she'd rather be a schoolteacher than marry for money, Elizabeth responds that Emma has no idea what it's like to be a poor teacher. Emma does, however, understand something of their situation when she remarks that "Female economy will do a great deal [...] but it cannot turn a small income into a large one".

The Watson women are visited by their insensitive lawyer brother, who is openly dismayed to find yet another sister thrown back on the family: alone with her dying clergyman father, Emma has some bleak thoughts about being important to no one and a burden to those on whose affection she cannot depend. Fortunately she has both intelligence and beauty, but the fragment ends before she can benefit from either. Austen family tradition records that she was to become dependent for "a home on her narrow-minded sister-in-law and brother", reject a lord and marry a gentlemanly clergyman, but it remains unclear how the other daughters were to be happily settled for the customary comic ending. Jane Austen kept the manuscript of "The Watsons" by her but never returned to finish or add to it. She made no fair copy.

Why did she stop writing? There are several possibilities. Her nephew James Edward Austen Leigh suggested she saw "the evil of having placed her heroine too low, in such a position of poverty and obscurity, as though not necessarily connected with vulgarity, has a sad tendency to degenerate into it". The subject matter was "unfavourable to the refinement of a lady". Since Austen went on to describe people in similar straitened circumstances in other novels, this may reflect Victorian rather than early nineteenth-century attitudes, but the accelerating revisions towards the end of the manuscript do indicate that she was having some trouble with her material.

Probably the main reason for her stopping – though not perhaps for never returning – was the sudden change in her circumstances: early in 1805 George Austen died. At that point correspondence between life and art may have become too close. In "The Watsons" a precipitating factor of the plot was to have been the cleric father's death, which would make his daughters thoroughly aware of their difficult financial status – as Jane and Cassandra must now have been. Jane's letters from this period treat the matter with mingled irony and bitterness: "prepare you[rself] for the sight of a Sister sunk in poverty, that it may not overcome your Spirits," she wrote to Cassandra. Another young woman found herself similarly unsupported, their friend Martha Lloyd whose mother died shortly after George Austen. She now joined the group of women in an arrangement so satisfactory it would last for the next two decades.

With George Austen's death, his income went to his son James. His widow and daughters had between them an annual income of £210, including the interest on Cassandra's legacy from Tom Fowle. It was neither secure nor sufficient for a genteel existence; consequently they had to look to the brothers for assistance: the wealthy landowner Edward, the banker Henry, and one of the sailor brothers, Frank. Each agreed to provide £50 a year, while Edward added another £100. The women quit the lodgings in Green Park Buildings. During his life or in his will George Austen had apparently made no effort to provide dowries for his daughters or provision for their lives as spinsters.

In the summer of 1806 they were in Clifton near Bristol. They then visited Stoneleigh and Steventon and, finally, Southampton. There they lodged for a while in Castle Square with Frank and his new wife Mary. Whatever she thought of her peripatetic life, Jane seems to have been glad to leave Bath and what she called in *Persuasion* its "white glare": on 1 July 1808 she wrote, "It will be two years tomorrow since we left Bath for Clifton, with what happy feelings of Escape!" She made many visits, some to Steventon again, to Chawton, and again to Godmersham where she enjoyed the "Elegance & Ease & Luxury", the pleasure of being "above Vulgar Economy" – though she seems not to have been such a favourite there as her sister Cassandra. She also visited London where Henry was living in some style with Eliza.

Maybe during this time Jane wrote and destroyed what she wrote, or she simply read and thought. Whatever the truth, she would emerge from these years a most extraordinary and powerful novelist.

7

Chawton

In 1809 Edward's wife died following childbirth. Jane and Cassandra helped to console some of the eleven motherless children, and their kindness at this difficult time seems to have prompted the widower into doing something more for his mother and sisters. Southampton had proved expensive and they were eager to move to cheaper and more secure lodgings.

Various possibilities were canvassed but, after considering villages near Edward or near Steventon, they settled on Chawton in Hampshire. They would live not in the manor house, which Edward only occasionally visited but otherwise let out to wealthy families or left vacant, but rather in a modest red-brick cottage by a fork on the main road. The house, which had formerly been a coaching inn and tavern, had six bedchambers, several garrets, a flower garden, space for vegetables, and a paddock in which to keep a donkey for a carriage.

Disappointed in a legacy they had hoped for from Mrs Austen's family, the women were relieved by this arrangement; they entered into their new life with mingled hope and resignation.

Jane was now thirty-three and had apparently "taken to the garb of middle age" rather early. She and her sister embraced again the kind of life they had lived at Steventon before their removal, although it could be difficult to attend the sort of social events – balls and assemblies – they had enjoyed fifteen years earlier. But Jane got over the "shame of being so much older" and declared herself "quite as happy now as then". She would never be free from "vulgar economy" and, with her mother, sister and friend, would concern herself with furniture, clothes, servants, washing days and all manner of domestic matters. She would also lead a full life of family visiting and being visited, watching the many children of the Austen brothers grow up, be launched and turn into agreeable or not so agreeable teenagers and adults. She especially came to delight in Edward's eldest girl Fanny, who began to show great interest in what her aunt was inventing and in the craft of writing. She worried over the sailor brothers, Francis and Charles, battling in the long war with France, and would be happy when she heard they were safe or had avoided a particularly bloody engagement.

Before she left Southampton she'd decided to nudge Crosby & Co. into publishing "Lady Susan". Assuming

JANE AUSTEN THE POET

Jane Austen loved the comedy of words and rhymes. She was a great admirer of poets such as William Cowper and George Crabbe, but she never attempted anything in their serious mode and, except for some verses in memory of a good friend, all her poems are light, even doggerel. Some form part of rhyming games and charades, some are occasional verse letters commemorating visits or family events. Others respond to comic news or incongruous names, as when Edward Foote marries Mary Patton or Mr Gell weds Miss Gill (he the slave of her "i.s" and she accepting his "e.s"). Only nineteen of probably numerous poems survive, almost all from the period between 1805 and 1812.

> *Our Chawton home –*
> *how much we find*
> *Already in it to our mind,*
> *And how convinced that*
> *when complete,*
> *It will all other Houses beat,*
> *That ever have been made or mended,*
> *With rooms concise or rooms distended.*

both marital and professional status, she wrote to the firm under the name of Mrs Ashton Dennis, "Authoress". The publishers had held on to the manuscript for six whole years and she concluded that such an amazingly long delay could only be due to their having lost the work. If this was the case, she would dispatch another copy – or, if they were uninterested in publishing, offer it elsewhere. Back came the reply from Crosby's son that she could have the manuscript returned "for the same as we paid for it": £10. It was a discouraging response and she let the matter rest there. For the moment she put the novel aside; when she returned to it years later, Susan would become Catherine, the heroine of *Northanger Abbey*.

Meanwhile she took up again the other two novels she had drafted in the 1790s: "Elinor and Marianne" and "First Impressions". The cancelled and rewritten chapters of *Persuasion*, as well as the revised pages of "The Watsons", reveal what her brother would later say of her, that she needed "many perusals" of her work before she was satisfied. She wrote, tried out and then rewrote. She was both a critical and a creative writer and each skill fed the other.

When Jane Austen achieved fame many years after her death, relatives and friends looked back on the author of the Chawton years. Cassandra remembered the lively discussions over the drafts of her stories – the two sisters were still the closest of companions and only with Cassandra would Jane talk "freely of any work that she might have in hand". Her nephew James Edward remembered a most virtuous aunt who was never impatient or irritable when the young nephews and nieces disturbed her at her work. Others recalled a more censorious and alarming figure, perhaps more in keeping with some of the caustic remarks in the letters and mordant asides of the narrators of the novels. The author Mary Russell Mitford repeated what her mother had told her of young Jane being the "prettiest, silliest, most affected husband-hunting butterfly" and how a friend declared she had "stiffened into the most perpendicular, precise, taciturn piece of 'single blessedness' that ever existed". Mitford went on: "a wit, a delineator of character, who does not talk, is terrific indeed".

8

The Professional Author

Settled at last in Chawton Cottage, Jane Austen became a professional writer. She'd overcome two publishing rebuffs: when her father offered an early manuscript to a bookseller and when she herself had uselessly sold "Lady Susan". Now she knew more and understood the value of her talent.

At her age she was unlikely to marry, and the only way to improve her financial position – and perhaps enhance her self-esteem and social status – was to write well for money. Fairly soon she would begin new projects, novels attuned to the troubled Regency years of George III's madness and an increasingly divided nation. But first she would revise those youthful works that had delighted her family in the

FANNY BURNEY (1752–1840)

Like Jane Austen, Fanny Burney started writing as a child in a large clever family. She was a prolific journal writer – her diary extends over seventy-two years. In 1778 she published her novel in letters *Evelina* to great acclaim; *Cecilia* followed in 1782. After an unhappy period as Second Keeper of the Robes to Queen Charlotte, she married a French émigré from the Revolution and had one son. To support the family she published *Camilla* in 1796. Fanny followed her husband to France in 1802 and was caught there when war with England resumed the following year. She returned to England in 1812 and published her final novel, *The Wanderer*, in 1814; it was her least successful work in terms of immediate reader response, but its vivid pictures of the difficulties of the unprotected woman in the marketplace and of the emotional woman who insists on her right to self-expression make it her most radical.

Burney's often very lengthy novels portray the adventures of young ladies brought up with good principles but with little understanding of the "world". They enter society and learn to behave in a "well-bred" way and to separate the false from the genuine; in the process of being trained, often almost to death, they find true love, usually with the man who has been their mentor or model – and sometimes tormentor. Austen was certainly influenced by this so-called entry plot, but she uses it more subtly than the often didactic and sensational Burney. She lets her heroines' moments of self-understanding come from ordinary events within the everyday world, while Burney's young women experience extremes of social and sexual disgrace, of illness and all kinds of suffering, which bring them close to mental breakdown. Only then do they completely discover their mistakes.

The title *Pride and Prejudice* probably alludes to the ending of Burney's *Cecilia*, where the miseries experienced by the hero and heroine are described as "the result of PRIDE and PREJUDICE".

previous century. When she had changed and corrected – but not updated – to her satisfaction, she would try to publish them. This time she meant to succeed.

She was going to market in a favourable climate. Throughout the eighteenth century the number of women novelists had been increasing, so that towards the end they had for a while actually become the majority – they would lose their ascendancy only in the 1820s. So to be a female author now was not unusual or daring, although publishing anonymously still remained common for a lady.

Novels were expensive to buy and were more cheaply

read through circulating libraries: readers were, Austen later lamented, "more ready to borrow & praise, than to buy". Her aim was to be the kind of author people invested in, writing books that were bought and prized, not simply borrowed and skimmed.

There were four possible ways to publish. A would-be author could sell the copyright and not worry about the production and marketing of the book. Or she could get a publisher to underwrite the cost and take a share of any profit. Or, if she had a wide circle of influential friends, she could get up a subscription to pay publication costs. Finally, she could do it herself: publish on commission, paying for printing, receiving profits (minus the publisher's 10 per cent cut) and accepting any loss. In 1803 with "Lady Susan" she'd tried the first option; for her second attempt in 1811 she would try the fourth. She had revised "Elinor and Marianne" into *Sense and Sensibility*: she would send this manuscript to be published on commission by the London publisher Thomas Egerton who, unlike Crosby, mainly specialized in political and military subjects. To her profound joy her proposal was accepted.

To publish in this risky manner she used money she had saved; she was further helped by Henry, who negotiated for her in London. Jane came up to town to correct proofs. Cassandra wrote to ask how the work was going: Jane might be too busy enjoying London to think of her book? "No indeed," responded Jane, "I am never too busy to think of S&S. I can no more forget it, than a mother can forget her sucking child." She'd been trying to get into print for fourteen years, and this, her first published novel, had been gestating for sixteen.

Sense and Sensibility made little stir in the literary world when it appeared in 1811, but its few reviews were satisfactory and it made a passable sum of money. The risk had paid off and she received £140 profit. Had she known what her success would be she might have tried the same with her next novel, but Egerton, presumably impressed with the modest sales, had already bought the copyright of *Pride and Prejudice* for £110. The sum was a little disappointing – she'd hoped for closer to £150 – but she took this method in part because of "great saving of Trouble to Henry". The decision was a financial error: costing 18s, this book became her most popular work and, had she published on commission, would have netted a goodly sum. On 29 January 1813 she received a printed copy of *Pride and Prejudice*, her "own darling Child". This second publication clarified her professional status, for the title page declared the novel "by the author of *Sense & Sensibility*".

Her limited but very real success delighted Jane Austen. The two novels together had earned £250 and she wrote excitedly to Francis that the welcome money "only makes me long for more". Her annual family income was small – by 1816 about £30 from government stock – and the money from novel writing – between £600 and £700 in total – was significant, even if it was nowhere near what the most celebrated women writers were earning: Fanny Burney received £4,000 for combined editions of *Camilla* and *The Wanderer*, and Maria Edgeworth £2,100 for *Patronage*.

And although her authorship was anonymous, success also brought some fame: "the Secret has spread so far as to be scarcely the Shadow of a secret now," she wrote, and she resolved that with the third book "I shall not even attempt to tell Lies about it. – I shall rather try to make all the Money than all the Mystery I can of it. – People shall pay for their Knowledge if I can make them." She had realized her contractual mistake with *Pride and Prejudice* and, when she came to sell the third work, the newly written *Mansfield Park,* Austen returned to publishing on commission. The book netted her £310, the most she would earn for a single novel. She was still with Egerton, but when he delayed putting out a second edition of a work she obviously valued highly – and possibly because she was ambitious for a more celebrated and literary publishing firm – she moved to John Murray, who dealt with such famous writers as Lord Byron and Walter Scott. She refused his offer of £450 for the copyright of *Sense and Sensibility*, *Mansfield Park* and a new novel, *Emma*, and again chose commission publishing.

It was another error. When Murray printed *Emma* along with a second edition of *Mansfield Park* in December 1815, Austen lost so much on the latter title that *Emma*, despite being her largest first edition at 2,000 copies, made her only £39. This was a sad state of affairs, especially since Henry was by now in financial difficulties. His siblings were involved in his banking crash and Jane herself lost about £25 from her profits.

But nothing long interfered with her astonishing creativity. She bought back "Lady Susan" from Crosby and began revising it. She also started on another novel, *Persuasion*. She would live to see neither published.

MARY WOLLSTONECRAFT

Mary Wollstonecraft was an Enlightenment feminist. Born to a feckless and increasingly impecunious father, she left home at a young age to become a companion, a teacher and a governess, none of which female roles suited her independent and assertive personality. After publishing a manual for educating girls, she took the bold step of becoming a professional writer, reviewing and authoring polemical works inspired by the radical political theories of the 1790s: *A Vindication of the Rights of Men* (1790) and *A Vindication of the Rights of Woman* (1792). In these works she argued for equality of educational opportunity for boys and girls and inveighed against the system of male primogeniture, depicted in its harmful effect on families in both *Sense and Sensibility* and *Pride and Prejudice*. Following an unhappy passion for the married artist and writer Henry Fuseli, she left for revolutionary France, where she fell in love with an American speculator who later abandoned her and their daughter. On his business she went to Scandinavia, then produced a lyrical work describing both her travels and her broken heart. She twice attempted suicide but finally found happiness with the radical philosopher William Godwin, whom she married just before her death following childbirth (her second daughter would become Mary Shelley, author of *Frankenstein*). Unwisely but lovingly, Godwin wrote a frank account of her life, describing her illegitimate child and suicide attempts.

9

Sense and Sensibility

When it was printed in 1811 a few critics applauded the morality of *Sense and Sensibility* but found it lacking in the sensational events they enjoyed in contemporary novels. Unaware that her aunt was the "Lady" of the title page, Jane Austen's niece Anna declared the novel "rubbish I am sure from the title". Other readers noted a "want of newness".

In truth it was perhaps a little old-fashioned, harking back to the moment of its conception rather than reflecting the time of its publication. Contrasting abstractions such as Nature and Art had been fashionable for titles in the 1790s but were less so by 1811 when single robust words like Discipline and Self-Control were more the mode. And the notion of sensibility certainly had greatest currency in the previous century when it was much used and abused across the cultural and political spectrum. Austen's treatment would appear to place her in the conservative camp, although she can never be tidily pigeonholed either politically or philosophically.

In *Sense and Sensibility* two young women, Elinor and Marianne (who is only sixteen), take on some aspects of the titular qualities. In *Northanger Abbey* Austen had portrayed Isabella Thorpe as an exploiter of sentiment, using emotional jargon with no real belief in it simply to promote her selfish ends. Marianne, however, is a more nuanced portrait of the power and pitfalls of sensibility, revealing how destructive the ideology can be within the mind of an essentially worthy young woman. Marianne loves disobeying conventional rules of propriety, for example by driving alone with an attractive man and visiting a house when the owner is absent: "if there had been any real impropriety in what I did, I should have been sensible of it at the time, for we always know when we are acting wrong," she protests. The older Elinor does not consider that a pleasant feeling must be a correct one.

Contrasted with warm sensibility is cold civility. The rather unpleasant society of the book is made tolerable only by superficial manners. After suffering from kindly, stupid people, Elinor bitterly reflects that sometimes "good breeding [is] more indispensable to comfort than good nature". Manners do not transform bad people, but they cover selfishness in a bleak world.

Also in stark contrast to sensibility – which at its best includes generosity of heart – is money, concupiscence and even prudence. W. H. Auden noted just how much Jane Austen was concerned with economic relations when he wrote:

> *It makes me most uncomfortable to see*
> *An English spinster of the middle-class*
> *Describe the amorous effects of "brass",*
> *Reveal so frankly and with such sobriety*
> *The economic basis of society.*

Sense and Sensibility is remarkably precise about sums of money. Its story revolves round their transmission and it satirizes family arrangements that financially disadvantage the worthy at the whim of the arrogant or unscrupulous, both men and women. An improvident father, an unkind will and a selfish half-brother reduce the Dashwood sisters from living on a country estate yielding £4,000 a year to lodging in a charitably provided cottage with £500 between them – a situation that painfully echoes that of the Austen women following George Austen's death. John Dashwood and his appalling wife Fanny see everything in terms of money and the property it brings. The selfishness they display appears even more dangerous than the self-centredness that may characterize sensibility. In one conversation, through mean but rational arguing, John allows a deathbed promise to his father of some £3,000 for his sisters to be whittled down to an occasional present. Fanny pictures the ensuing life of the unattached women: without carriage or horses, with hardly any servants and no company, "how comfortable they will be". This is far removed from the kindly but prudent "sense" Elinor displays.

THE CULT OF SENSIBILITY

Sensibility as an idea and cult was based on the assumption that people were born not innately corrupted, as religion taught, but innately good. If undamaged, they could remain virtuous. Consequently the need for rigid external rules of conduct disappeared and an individual could trust to intuition: if it *felt* right, it must *be* right. The body acting spontaneously and uncontrollably expressed truth – blushing, palpitating, shivering or crying. Medical theories which stressed the importance of the nervous system supported emphasis on the body's power over the mind and, since it was so involved with the body, sensibility became associated with women regarded as especially at the mercy of bodily impulses; their frailty could be applauded as refinement and sensitivity.

By emphasizing responsive feeling, the Cult of Sensibility could promote self-absorption. The philosopher David Hume, who theorized the cultural fashion, wrote:

Some people are subject to a certain delicacy of passion, which makes them extremely sensible to all the accidents of life, and gives them a lively joy upon every prosperous event, as well as a piercing grief, when they meet with misfortunes and adversity [...] [M]en of such lively passions are apt to be transported beyond all bounds of prudence and discretion, and to take false steps in the conduct of life, which are often irretrievable.

Inevitably moralists, particularly those writing conduct books for young women, feared where all this might lead: they urged girls not to trust either their own emotions or the emotional and seductive protestations of men.

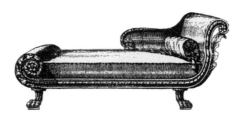

10

Two Heroines: Elinor and Marianne

I n *Sense and Sensibility*, uniquely in Jane Austen's published novels, there are two heroines. Elinor and Marianne echo the contrasting pairs in works of the period, for example Elizabeth Inchbald's *Simple Story* (1791) or Jane West's *A Gossip's Story* (1796). West's novel pits the beautiful, romantic but rather spoilt Marianne against the reserved and more sensible Louisa.

Sense and Sensibility only superficially recalls these often schematic works, and the apparent contrast of Elinor and Marianne collapses on closer or repeated reading. Both heroines develop into rounded characters and together they examine the big question of the individual's relationship to her society, asking how we live without succumbing to its trivial standards, how we "tell lies when politeness requires it" or, rejecting what seems hypocrisy, avoid growing morose through its apparent cruelty. Individual and society always oppose each other, it seems, but society can also help and nurture – as long as necessary pretence does not become downright duplicity. There must be negotiation.

In the novel, Elinor by no means always acts through reason and Marianne is not always impulsive. When Marianne receives the letter of rejection from her beloved Willoughby she becomes deathly pale; Elinor trembles. As she reads, Marianne collapses – she "almost choaked", then "almost screamed"; Elinor gives "way to a burst of tears, which at first were scarcely less violent than Marianne's". The two heroines do differ, however. When lovers disappoint, Marianne loses all control in public, Elinor acts with caution. As a result one has to suffer the pity of strangers, the other receives none and is glad of it. Marianne responds to rejection by falling ill and nearly dying, so causing immense suffering to her loving family. Elinor's stoical but deep feeling is beautifully caught in the passage describing her response to her sister's recovery:

Elinor could not be cheerful. Her joy was of a different kind, and led to anything rather than to gaiety. Marianne restored to life, health, friends, and to her doating mother, was an idea to fill her heart with sensations of exquisite comfort, and expand it in fervent gratitude; – but it led to no outward demonstration of joy, no words, no smiles. All within Elinor's breast was satisfaction, silent and strong.

Sense and Sensibility shows that sentimental romance, nurtured by cultural expectations, is less valuable in life than slow developing love. Desire is less a guarantor of happiness than an esteem that in the end can incorporate self-esteem.

Yet many readers have preferred the impulsive and enthusiastic Marianne to her cautious sister. Princess Charlotte, the Prince Regent's fifteen-year-old daughter, found some comfort in the picture: "I think Marianne & me are very like in *disposition*, that certainly I am not so good, the same imprudence, &tc." The ending, which seemed to coerce Marianne into a prudential match, disturbed some early readers. "[I]t ends stupidly," remarked Lady Bessborough, who otherwise was "much amused" by the novel. In the twentieth century the critic Marvin Mudrick sternly declared that Marianne was "betrayed; and not by Willoughby".

Even more of a contrast than the heroines are the men they love: Edward, secretly engaged to a vulgar woman, is plain, diffident, retiring, said to be good at heart, and extraordinarily weak in his dealings with women, including his mother; he is Elinor's brother-in-law, so already part of the extended family. Willoughby is all that a young man should be, handsome, glamorous and sexually alluring – the contemporary *British Critic* called him "a male coquet" – and he arrives out of the storm and into their lives in the most romantic way, scooping up Marianne and entering her heart. Colonel Brandon, with whom Marianne must be satisfied, seems grave and feels much older, but he has the most romantic past, including a dead beloved and her fallen daughter.

Minor characters duplicate the main actors. The vulgar sisters Lucy and Anne Steele have even more need to marry than the Dashwood women, but they go about it with less refinement. Lady Middleton and Mrs Palmer are contrasting daughters of the irritating, talkative but kindly Mrs Jennings: the first is all cold decorum, the other silly merriment.

In her letters Jane Austen makes the kind of astringent remarks about irritating neighbours, adultery, dead babies and unloved husbands that no heroine would be allowed to utter. In *Northanger Abbey* the reader saw young Catherine through the amused eyes of the novel's narrator. Similarly here, Marianne is often the butt of sardonic remarks from the narrator for her romantic attitudes and unrealistic enthusiasms. Very frequently in *Sense and Sensibility* the narrator inhabits Elinor's mind – far more than Marianne's – and often it is unclear whether wry or even waspish thoughts are hers or Elinor's (though Elinor does not completely escape the narrator's irony in the novel – witness her self-deceiving attitudes to both Edward and Willoughby where indeed she may on occasion show what she describes: a "total misapprehension of character"). As Edward's trivial brother Robert Ferrars is buying a toothpick case in a London shop he stares broadly at Elinor, whom he keeps waiting; his crude display of masculine vacuity irritates her. He's said to have a face "of strong, natural, sterling insignificance". The narrator's comment, or Elinor's, or both?

Like its successor *Sense and Sensibility* is a novel that suggests that people, along with books, require more than one perusal and that not all secrets are ever completely revealed.

EXTRACT FROM *SENSE AND SENSIBILITY*

They gaily ascended the downs, rejoicing in their own penetration at every glimpse of blue sky; and when they caught in their faces the animating gales of an high south-westerly wind, they pitied the fears which had prevented their mother and Elinor from sharing such delightful sensations.

"Is there a felicity in the world," said Marianne, "superior to this? — Margaret, we will walk here at least two hours."

Margaret agreed, and they pursued their way against the wind, resisting it with laughing delight for about twenty minutes longer, when suddenly the clouds united over their heads, and a driving rain set full in their face. — Chagrined and surprised, they were obliged, though unwillingly, to turn back, for no shelter was nearer than their own house. One consolation however remained for them, to which the exigence of the moment gave more than usual propriety; it was that of running with all possible speed down the steep side of the hill which led immediately to their garden gate.

They set off. Marianne had at first the advantage, but a false step brought her suddenly to the ground, and Margaret, unable to stop herself to assist her, was involuntarily hurried along, and reached the bottom in safety.

A gentleman carrying a gun, with two pointers playing round him, was passing up the hill and within a few yards of Marianne, when her accident happened. He put down his gun and ran to her assistance. She had raised herself from the ground, but her foot had been twisted in the fall, and she was scarcely able to stand. The gentleman offered his services, and perceiving that her modesty declined what her situation rendered necessary, took her up in his arms without farther delay, and carried her down the hill. Then passing through the garden, the gate of which had been left open by Margaret, he bore her directly into the house, whither Margaret was just arrived, and quitted not his hold till he had seated her in a chair in the parlour.

Elinor and her mother rose up in amazement at their entrance, and while the eyes of both were fixed on him with an evident wonder and a secret admiration which equally sprung from his appearance, he apologized for his intrusion by relating its cause, in a manner so frank and so graceful, that his person, which was uncommonly handsome, received additional charms from his voice and expression. Had he been even old, ugly, and vulgar, the gratitude and kindness of Mrs. Dashwood would have been secured by any act of attention to her child; but the influence of youth, beauty, and elegance, gave an interest to the action which came home to her feelings.

She thanked him again and again; and with a sweetness of address which always attended her, invited him to be seated. But this he declined, as he was dirty and wet. Mrs. Dashwood then begged to know to whom she was obliged. His name, he replied, was Willoughby, and his present home was at Allenham, from whence he hoped she would allow him the honour of calling to-morrow to inquire after Miss Dashwood. The honour was readily granted, and he then departed, to make himself still more interesting, in the midst of an heavy rain.

11

Pride and Prejudice

While *Sense and Sensibility* was being printed, Jane Austen was revising a work started almost fifteen years earlier: *Pride and Prejudice*. The openings of the two novels could not have differed more, the one cumbersome, explaining the Dashwood family estate and relationships, the other spare, giving little away of the setting or future plot but pulling the reader firmly into the novel – the novel that would become her most approved work in her lifetime and long after her death one of the world's most popular romances.

Austen did not need to make substantial changes to the social background. The French wars dragged on and the military men who entered her pages in the later 1790s were still there in 1813. So her revisions were mainly formal, a matter of condensing. She "lopt & cropt", making a taut text with few details of person or place. She intended what she later called "the playfulness & Epigrammatism of the general style". When she was done she described her novel with ironic pride as possibly rather too "light & bright & sparkling". Perhaps she could have copied more learned writers and padded out this brilliant work with some "solemn specious nonsense", possibly "an Essay on Writing, a critique on Walter Scott, or the history of Buonaparte". She was sure that fiction needed to be entertaining and readable. She knew hers was both.

There is much realism in *Pride and Prejudice*, much probability in character. While the hero is suitably passionate, the lady is cooler: Elizabeth Bennet fancies two charming soldiers before realizing where her interest – and heart – lies. "If gratitude and esteem are good foundations of affection, Elizabeth's change of sentiment will be neither improbable nor faulty," remarks the prosaic narrator, who endorses her method of avoiding instant romance and seeking the "less interesting mode of attachment". Yet this novel is as near as Austen comes to fantasy and romance. *Pride and Prejudice* heads a long tradition of romantic fiction of the Cinderella type, in which a more humble girl captures and tames a rich, powerful, overbearing man. Darcy is the wealthiest of her leading men, the nearest to aristocracy and to later romantic heroes such as *Jane Eyre*'s Mr Rochester or *Rebecca*'s Maxim de Winter. Charlotte Brontë wrote that Austen avoided the passions, that she rejected "even a speaking acquaintance with that stormy Sisterhood". Most admirers of Mr Darcy disagree.

The traditional romantic heroine lacks parents and siblings; Austen's heroine is one of five spirited and unmarried daughters, all "silly and ignorant" in their father's cynical view. Elizabeth Bennet is vital and cheerful. She can be critical, both of her friend Charlotte when she disappoints her in seeking only comfort in marriage, and even of her father when he inappropriately indulges his sardonic humour. But mainly she is simply sceptical, wry and sharp, finding amusing those vacuous conversations that so frustrated Marianne and accepting with Mr Bennet that we live "but to make sport for our neighbours, and laugh at them in our turn". Readers have fallen in love with Elizabeth; Austen herself wrote, "I must confess that I think her as delightful a creature as ever appeared in print".

To some extent Elizabeth's maturing involves curbing this attractive spiritedness and moving from one male influence to another; it is the grave Darcy, not her amusing father, who saves the family by rescuing sister Lydia from becoming a fallen woman and taking them all down with her disgrace. Although never quite repressed, to become the wife of a haughty man and chatelaine of a great house Elizabeth has to curtail the wit her father encouraged; she admits "my spirits might often lead me wrong". When she encounters Darcy at a ball where she'd hoped to meet the dashing Wickham, like Henry Tilney with the naive Catherine she takes control of the discourse and tries to form herself and Darcy into the theatrical pair of witty lovers, but Darcy cannot rise to such sprightliness; at stuffy Rosings, when her interest falls on Darcy's cousin, she's pert and comic. Yet when she sees Darcy at Pemberley she's "astonished and confused", embarrassed to appear a middle-class tourist accompanied by relatives he might scorn; later she's discomposed when she views him and his sister from the inn, and when she tells him of Lydia's elopement her knees tremble and she bursts into tears.

Like Lydia, Elizabeth had in the early pages laughed a lot. When Miss Bingley announces that Darcy is not to be laughed at, she ridicules the notion: "That is an uncommon advantage, and uncommon I hope it will continue, for it would be a great loss to me to have many such acquaintance. I dearly love a laugh." But at the end of the novel she knows Darcy "had yet to learn to be laught at." (Laughter is closely associated with sexy Lydia, who elopes with Wickham leaving a note which reads: "You will laugh when you know where I am gone, and I cannot help laughing myself at your surprise to-morrow morning, as soon as I am missed.")

Almost grotesquely arrogant in the early pages, Darcy is perhaps more attractive on screen – where he can express his real and growing passion with smouldering looks – than in the novel, which stays largely within Elizabeth's viewpoint. He is initially too proud of his rank; he learns civility only when Elizabeth bridles at the insult to her family's lower status and herself and he comes to understand that to be a gentleman requires more than cleverness, wealth and status. However, although his proposal is insulting, the first words of the untamed Darcy are thrilling: "You must allow me to tell you how ardently I admire and love you."

Beyond its beguiling romance, *Pride and Prejudice* is a wonderfully comic story of family embarrassment: Mr Collins with his pride in his absurdly bossy patron Lady Catherine and his inept, insistent proposal to his cousin; Mrs Bennet, with her nerves and ebullient vulgarity; Mary with her boring piano-playing. The book displays brilliant set pieces of social shame: "to Elizabeth it appeared, that had her family made an agreement to expose themselves as much as they could during the evening, it would have been impossible for them to play their parts with more spirit, or finer success". Naughtily, her father enjoys such scenes – so do readers.

EXTRACT FROM *PRIDE AND PREJUDICE*

Elizabeth Bennet has just received a proposal from Mr Collins, her odious cousin and heir to their property. She has refused it, to her mother's horror and her sardonic father's delight.

She would not give him time to reply, but hurrying instantly to her husband, called out as she entered the library, "Oh! Mr. Bennet, you are wanted immediately; we are all in an uproar. You must come and make Lizzy marry Mr. Collins, for she vows she will not have him, and if you do not make haste he will change his mind and not have *her*."

Mr. Bennet raised his eyes from his book as she entered, and fixed them on her face with a calm unconcern which was not in the least altered by her communication.

"I have not the pleasure of understanding you," said he, when she had finished her speech. "Of what are you talking?"

"Of Mr. Collins and Lizzy. Lizzy declares she will not have Mr. Collins, and Mr. Collins begins to say that he will not have Lizzy."

"And what am I to do on the occasion? — It seems an hopeless business."

"Speak to Lizzy about it yourself. Tell her that you insist upon her marrying him."

"Let her be called down. She shall hear my opinion."

Mrs. Bennet rang the bell, and Miss Elizabeth was summoned to the library.

"Come here, child," cried her father as she appeared. "I have sent for you on an affair of importance. I understand that Mr. Collins has made you an offer of marriage. Is it true?" Elizabeth replied that it was. "Very well — and this offer of marriage you have refused?"

"I have, Sir."

"Very well. We now come to the point. Your mother insists upon your accepting it. Is not it so, Mrs. Bennet?"

"Yes, or I will never see her again."

"An unhappy alternative is before you, Elizabeth. From this day you must be a stranger to one of your parents. — Your mother will never see you again if you do *not* marry Mr. Collins, and I will never see you again if you *do*."

12

Man of Property: Darcy and Pemberley

Pride and Prejudice is a novel of houses: Longbourn, Netherfield, Hunsford, Rosings – and of course Pemberley. Great houses always feature in Jane Austen's novels. The first published work, *Sense and Sensibility*, opens with her heroines being ejected from a great house; the last, *Persuasion*, starts with the heroine likewise being forced out but ends with her choosing not to return, instead embracing a rootless life. But no novel treats a house quite as *Pride and Prejudice* treats Pemberley.

Unlike many early poets of country houses and contemporary novelists using setting to deliver characters, Austen does not straightforwardly equate a home with its owner, though she may let her heroines make such connections. Noisy

87

Longbourn and vacant Netherfield do not signify particular qualities. Rosings appears ridiculous when Mr Collins rhapsodizes, but in fact the insolent and rude Lady Catherine does not have an entirely pretentious house and estate: "Every park has its beauty and its prospects; and Elizabeth saw much to be pleased with, though she could not be in such raptures as Mr. Collins expected the scene to inspire." Unlike Ann Radcliffe or Fanny Burney, Austen gives us little detail of place, and her minimalism is quite intended: when her niece Anna showed her some of her writing, she responded, "your descriptions are often more minute than will be liked". Details are for mundane conversation only, and when Elizabeth and Darcy, feeling awkward, finally talk of Matlock and Dove Dale, we don't hear what they say.

Even Pemberley is not much described except in generalized terms, although its effect on Elizabeth is powerfully conveyed. Before seeing it she had signalled interest in "that noble place", which Bingley declares beyond any match. After the surprise proposal from Darcy she accompanies her aunt and uncle on a tour of Derbyshire. (In the eighteenth century visitors of the upper and middle ranks became tourists of great houses and grounds; they expected to be shown around by the housekeeper and gardener.) One of the sights is Pemberley. Women do a lot of looking in Austen's novels, mainly at men; here Elizabeth looks closely at a house, and man and property do inevitably appear entwined. Darcy is not yet clearly an object of love; yet she finds "her spirits […] in a high flutter" when she approaches his home:

It was a large, handsome, stone building, standing well on
rising ground, and backed by a ridge of high woody hills;
– and in front, a stream of some natural importance was
swelled into greater, but without any artificial appearance.
Its banks were neither formal, nor falsely adorned. Elizabeth
was delighted. She had never seen a place for which nature
had done more, or where natural beauty had been so little
counteracted by an awkward taste. They were all of them
warm in their admiration; and at that moment she felt,
that to be mistress of Pemberley might be something!

This famous, slightly comic ending to the rhapsody is in
keeping with Elizabeth's droll assertion to Jane, who has
enquired when her sister changed her dislike of Darcy into
esteem and love, that it was on "first seeing his beautiful
grounds at Pemberley".

The new Darcy emerges for Elizabeth through images:
the house itself, the estate, the housekeeper's discourse and
the portrait. He had started the book as an insolent man
who strutted about a provincial ball "fancying himself so
very great" (in Mrs Bennet's critical words). But now he
gains glamour from images that are positive, appealing,
strangely indistinct, as well as from his association with
the heroine. Before she set off on her tour Elizabeth had
determined to remember and describe in detail. But in
fact Pemberley just settles in her consciousness in general
terms, allowing the master to merge with his aesthetically
pleasing possessions and worthy duties. It appears a
resounding conversion of the once sceptical heroine,

proud of her middling rank, to what the great conservative apologist of the revolutionary period, Edmund Burke, calls our cherished "old prejudices" in favour of stability, stasis and hierarchy. Fitzwilliam Darcy, the nearest to an aristocrat with a major role in an Austen novel, has the best taste and is simply "the best landlord, and the best master [...] that ever lived". His power is to conserve and maintain, to keep rooms, rivers and library well stocked and tenants happy.

From her father's farming days and the concerns of her landowning relatives, Jane Austen was well aware of agricultural issues; indeed, from the later novels a modern reader could learn something of how English country estates were managed. But no economic details ruffle the calm perfection of heritage Pemberley. No wonder "gentle sensations" come over Elizabeth when she thinks "how many people's happiness were in [Darcy's] guardianship". The offer of his hand has become the offer of a fine estate and a traditional way of life: Elizabeth now thinks of "his regard with a deeper sentiment of gratitude than it had ever raised before". From being the daughter of a man who possessed a small mansion only in his lifetime and had horses doing duty for farming and leisure, she could become chatelaine of a great house possessed securely, resplendently – and vaguely – by its owner. Happily this owner learns to modify his noble "prejudices" and be "humbled"; he finds that life with the unconventional Elizabeth and sometimes with her trading relatives, the excellent but formerly despised Gardiners, will help deliver him from the Pemberley stasis and any sense that this marriage of equals is a "degradation".

THE REAL PEMBERLEY

There is no one accepted original of Pemberley
but there has been much speculation. Austen
especially knew Godmersham and Stoneleigh,
both connected with her family, but Chatsworth in
Derbyshire, mentioned in the novel, is often put
forward as a model. Although this seat of the Dukes
of Devonshire may be rather too grand even for
Darcy, Austen adaptations on screen do favour the
magnificent – so Chatsworth was used for the 2005
film. Lyme Park in Cheshire was used for the 1995
BBC version. The 1940 film, made during the lean
years of the Second World War, did not feature a
great house at all.

13

War and Peace

Almost all of Jane Austen's life was spent in a country at war – and war accelerates change. So the period when she was sketching out her first three novels – the revolutionary 1790s – is radically different from the later one – the Regency – when she was publishing the finished works and composing the final three.

The two great revolutions – the political French and the industrial British – profoundly affected the nation in which she lived. The Britain that emerged into peace in 1815 was the world's first urban industrial power. It valued entrepreneurial and technological advance while distrusting radical political change and abstract ideals. It now associated these with the Continental Europe against which it had struggled for so long.

When the extreme faction of the French Revolution, the Jacobins, had gained power in Paris in 1793, a Reign of Terror against aristocracy and opponents had begun. War between Britain and France was declared and, with brief cessations in 1802 and 1814, would continue until only a couple of years before Jane Austen's death. The French and Napoleonic Wars do not dominate her novels, but she allows glimpses of them throughout, and the army and militia come to the fore in *Pride and Prejudice,* and the navy in *Mansfield Park* and especially *Persuasion,* which is set just before final hostilities ceased.

In the 1790s and early 1800s Britain seemed unprepared for battling an expansionist power like Revolutionary France. The royal dukes, with little military or professional skill, were often in charge of forces fighting on enemy terrain they barely understood. After various setbacks abroad, a nervous government cracked down with so-called "Gagging Acts" on home-grown British radical and liberal writers, now branded unpatriotic French sympathizers. As the years passed, and French Terror yielded to the imperial dictatorship of Napoleon, a new British nationalism emerged, based on King, Country and Church.

A rather lax and worldly organization in the eighteenth century, the Church of England now found its ascendancy threatened by more serious and forceful evangelical movements on its flank. Difficult political times required from the state religion a sterner, more moral response than it had given in earlier decades. The younger Jane Austen did not favour enthusiastic worship and always adhered to the established church, but towards the end of the long war years she came to understand that evangelicalism answered a national need. In her final novels both the Church and the Royal Navy are presented as serious callings, although her attitude is, as usual, never simple or absolutely secure. In *Mansfield Park* Henry Crawford at one moment imagines "the glory of heroism, of usefulness, of exertion, of endurance" that military life could bring, and at another the theatrical gratification of being a London preacher; he then concludes that the life of a rich leisured gentleman is preferable to either.

Jane Austen was personally connected to the war through her family. She wrote of the deaths of British soldiers at the battle of Corunna in 1809, "We have had no one to care for particularly among the Troops", but she cared deeply for the sufferings and dangers of her two naval brothers, whom she both loved and greatly admired. Her letters to Francis in particular are full of respect as well as affection.

Francis had joined Nelson in 1798 and was part of the pursuit of Napoleon after the Battle of the Nile. He was also present at the blockading of the French fleet which threatened Britain and he accompanied convoys to Africa and the West Indies. Sadly in his view, he just missed being part of the action at Trafalgar in 1805 – a hugely welcome event in an England desperately in need of a resounding victory. Charles was equally active, capturing enemy boats first around the North American coasts and then in the Mediterranean and Adriatic. Jane read and reread the letters of both sailor brothers and scoured newspapers for information of their engagements.

By 1814 it appeared that Britain and her allies had defeated the French both at sea and on land, and the big bogeyman Napoleon was exiled to Elba. It was a short-lived peace. Napoleon soon escaped to France, and so great was his charisma – and so unpopular the royalist regime established in his place – that he was able to recapture Paris and restart the war. The British were aghast. Renewed fighting followed, and in June 1815 the Duke of Wellington, a soldier whose military heroism on land matched that of Nelson at sea, helped defeat Napoleon for the last time: the long conflict was finally over.

Britain finished the Napoleonic Wars as a major European power – a fact that gave no joy to liberal thinkers who saw the old order and hierarchies re-established in devastated countries or to the English poor who hadn't benefited from the high agricultural prices of the war years. Austen herself could never have approved of the conflict, and yet her novels testify to the useful fluidity of class that became possible in wartime, when military men of spirit and ambition could rise to take on the estates of incompetent gentry.

14

Mansfield Park

Jane Austen was aware that *Mansfield Park* was "not half so entertaining" as *Pride and Prejudice*, but she was ambitious and never wished to repeat a formula. Although she was revising the earlier novel while writing the later one, there's little cross-fertilization: both are romances, but *Mansfield Park* raises questions of selfhood and political and personal responsibility, passion and repression, that are not easily answered; despite the conclusion of marriage, there's a lingering sense of melancholy what-might-have-been. It was the only one of Austen's novels to have no review in a literary periodical.

The novel is troubling and uncomfortable and, although it has many comic moments, it's mostly serious in theme and dialogue.

Readers who are disappointed or discomfited by *Mansfield Park* primarily blame the heroine, Fanny Price, regarded by some as priggish and judgemental, and marked with a physical weakness that suits her victim status. The problem is compounded by her foil, Mary Crawford. Lacking Fanny's grave moral sense, Mary echoes in more risqué fashion the witty remarks that enlivened the conversation of Elizabeth Bennet, and her spirit and impudence seem on the whole more attractive to a modern reader than Fanny's apparent submissiveness. Mary throws herself wholeheartedly into the amateur theatricals at Mansfield – the sort that had, when Jane was a child, delighted the Austens and their lively cousin Eliza de Feuillide but which to Fanny appear morally and socially perilous in the absence of the head of the family.

Austen left "The Watsons" unfinished, but with *Mansfield Park* she returned to its plot in describing a girl plucked out of her home, genteelly educated, then forced to return to a far less affluent family to face not only their straitened economic existence but also the vulgarity it delivered – a vulgarity that's painful and constricting and much less comic than the ebullient vulgarity of the Bennets in *Pride and Prejudice*. Unlike Elizabeth Bennet or Elinor and Marianne Dashwood, Fanny Price is seen in childhood, expressing childish fears and wants. Her removals signify crises in her life: the frightened arrival of the child at Mansfield Park and the young woman's disappointing return to her greasy Portsmouth home. This latter removal occurs when the eligible Henry Crawford decides it would be a challenge to stop flirting with Maria Bertram, who loves him, and instead seduce her cousin, the mousey Fanny, who is seemingly of little account in the Mansfield family. Henry is a mixed character, vain and cruel from one angle, clever and morally astute from another, both aware of his gentlemanly privilege and corrupted by that privilege and by wrong example. Fanny's very reserve and modesty – so different from the self-assurance of girls of his own rank – together with her devotion to her naval brother, work on him, and he begins to see in her the qualities of a wife; his aim moves from seduction to wooing.

Presuming on his attractive status, he makes known his wish to her uncle Sir Thomas, who assumes that marriage so much above his niece's expectations must be welcome, especially to a girl who's shown herself obedient and seemingly more attentive to his will than his own spoilt daughters. But he encounters Fanny's secret love for his son Edmund and her stern moral sense, her repugnance at Henry's earlier flirting throughout the theatricals with the engaged Maria. Knowing the value of a luxurious home, Sir Thomas returns Fanny to her original family to become "heartily sick" of indigence and to yearn for the comforts Henry's large income can bring.

Fanny goes to Portsmouth with mistaken expectations of being "in the centre of such a circle, loved by so many, and more loved by all than she had ever been before" and of feeling "affection without fear or restraint". It's the fantasy of a neglected child, and when it is swiftly punctured by reality her judgement is as stern on her mother as it was on Henry Crawford: Mrs Price is "a dawdle, a slattern [...] who had no talent, no conversation, no affection towards herself". So Fanny becomes a little fonder of Henry and a great deal more of the once unwelcoming Mansfield Park, now seen as the heavenly place to Portsmouth's domestic hell. Sir Thomas is right: the greasy furniture and dreadful puddings do his work for him. But Fanny is saved from compromise by the unstable Henry, who cannot sustain his new character and elopes with the always willing Maria. The adultery is flippantly seen as a social mistake by Mary Crawford, who appals the clerical Edmund with her attitude; to Fanny it's "too horrible a confusion of guilt, too gross a complication of evil, for human nature, not in a state of utter barbarism, to be capable of!" It's a fortunate fall, however, for it leads to her achievement of Edmund. She returns to become the centre of Mansfield Park instead of Portsmouth.

"I do not quite know what to make of Miss Fanny. I do not understand her [...] What is her character? – Is she solemn? – Is she queer? – Is she prudish?" muses Henry Crawford when he decides on his emotional assault. Some critics see her as a Christlike figure come to redeem the estate. However, this is probably putting too much weight on one aspect of a complex and flawed character. Her path is indeed more fraught, and her thoughts more serious, than those of other Austen heroines, and she is passionate and excessive underneath the prim covering. Her introspection causes her constantly to investigate herself and her motives, and, in her rhapsodies about nature and poetry, she seems more spiritual than her predecessors. But she is also a little absurd. She's jealous and competitive, often wilfully pathetic with her "sore and angry heart", and then "exquisitely happy" when everyone else is plunged into misery. Fanny Price is no ideal then, but rather a struggling soul learning self-reliance, with an active but sometimes painful sense of duty which wars with her desires.

A THIEF IN THE FAMILY?

The Portsmouth scene might recall Jane Austen's memories of her wealthy aunt Jane Leigh-Perrot's experiences. In August 1799 Mrs Leigh-Perrot entered a Bath linen-draper's to buy black lace. When she left, the shopkeeper insisted on inspecting her parcel. A card of white lace, worth 20 shillings, was discovered. The clerk must have mistakenly packed it with her black lace, Mrs Leigh-Perrot asserted; the shopkeeper called her a thief. A few days later she was arrested.

Held for eight months awaiting the March Assizes, because of her status and wealth, she was lodged with the gaoler's slovenly family; her devoted husband accompanied her, experiencing:

"Vulgarity, Dirt, Noise from morning till night [...] Cleanliness has ever been his greatest delight, and yet he sees the greasy toast laid by the dirty children on his knees, and feels the small Beer trickle down his Sleeves on its way across the table unmoved."

Probably Jane Austen was relieved when Mrs Leigh-Perrot refused her mother's offer of sending her daughters to keep their aunt company. Since the punishment for theft was most likely deportation to Botany Bay for fourteen years, the couple made plans for Mr Leigh-Perrot to sell his properties and follow his wife. But when the trial took place on 29 March 1800 the jury found Mrs Leigh-Perrot "not guilty".

Was the affair a matter of blackmail, or of justice being perverted by status (and the severity of the punishment)?

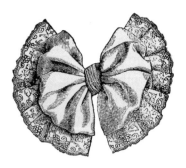

15

Licence and Restraint:
the Moral World of
Mansfield Park

It is not absolutely clear when Jane Austen began *Mansfield Park*, in 1811 or 1812, but she finished it in summer 1813. So it was written entirely during the Napoleonic Wars, when the nation was in serious mood, fearful of French invasion and aware of growing social problems at home. It is possibly no accident that *Mansfield Park* shares its name with the famous judge, Lord Mansfield, so controversial for his disruptive ruling in 1772 which made slavery illegal on English soil.

Many writers called for a new moral purpose in state and church, an ideology to pull the nation and its ranks together and make it worthy of victory. The discussions concerning education and religion in the novel occur in this context. The result is a more earnest novel than any Austen published before or after.

Mary Wollstonecraft had wanted a more rational and rigorously intellectual education for girls and boys. Austen was unconvinced: she mocked Mary Bennet's efforts to educate herself in *Pride and Prejudice*, and the fact-based learning of the Bertram girls, which persuades them of their superiority to their ignorant cousin Fanny, is even less useful. Maria and Julia Bertram have civil manners and factual knowledge but lack any innate sense of duty: they have no firm principles.

The morality necessary for the nation's wellbeing was best supported by the Church of England, but only when that Church was cleansed of its association with eighteenth-century laxity and selfishness. In a letter of 29 January 1813 Jane told Cassandra, "Now I will try to write of something else; – it shall be a complete change of subject – Ordination." This appears to be written after *Mansfield Park* was begun and is probably part of a query about clerical training. However, it can be argued that "ordination" is important in this novel. In the earlier books, clergymen are comic, as Mr Collins or men-about-town like Henry Tilney. Edmund Bertram is far more serious: he believes that a clergyman "has the charge of all that is of the first importance to mankind, individually or collectively considered, temporally and eternally, [he] has the guardianship of religion and morals, and consequently of the manners which result from their influence."

His father echoes him when he remarks that a clergyman must reside in his parish: "human nature needs more lessons than a weekly sermon can convey". The message is clear: "as the clergy are, or are not what they ought to be, so are the rest of the nation".

Sir Thomas Bertram might add that, as landowners are, so are the citizens of a nation. He wants to be the moral centre of his estate, Mansfield Park, but his own ambitions, his probable involvement in slave-owning in Antigua, and his lack of imagination – he marries the stupidest of women for her beauty, judges his passionate daughter unemotional, believes good-intentioned tyranny can be appreciated, and feels a radical distinction between rich and poor – mean that he fails to give three of his four children a proper ethical education. By the end of the book he comes to see that a person needs to struggle to gain firm principles and – what he had not known at the outset – that no one should be judged by his or her monetary value.

His is the fault of the culture in general: *Mansfield Park* opens with three sisters being presented solely as commodities for marriage. All three make unions that are unsatisfactory for the next generation: marrying simply for love is no better than marrying for status and gain. Prudence and affection need to be in balance, esteem is as important as love. The happy ending comes about only when Edmund and Fanny, two principled children of two inadequate mothers, are united. To preserve purity the unprincipled child Maria has to be exiled and punished.

Because of his spendthrift heir, Sir Thomas must see to

EXTRACT FROM *MANSFIELD PARK*

Maria and Henry Crawford are in the Sotherton grounds, supposedly waiting for Maria's betrothed to fetch the key to the gate.

"Your prospects...are too fair to justify want of spirits. You have a very smiling scene before you."

"Do you mean literally or figuratively? Literally, I conclude. Yes, certainly, the sun shines, and the park looks very cheerful. But unluckily that iron gate, that ha-ha, give me a feeling of restraint and hardship. 'I cannot get out,' as the starling said." As she spoke, and it was with expression, she walked to the gate; he followed her. "Mr. Rushworth is so long fetching this key!"

"And for the world you would not get out without the key and without Mr. Rushworth's authority and protection, or I think you might with little difficulty pass round the edge of the gate, here, with my assistance; I think it might be done, if you really wished to be more at large, and could allow yourself to think it not prohibited."

"Prohibited! nonsense! I certainly can get out that way, and I will. Mr. Rushworth will be here in a moment, you know — we shall not be out of sight."

"Or if we are, Miss Price will be so good as to tell him that he will find us near that knoll, the grove of oak on the knoll."

> Fanny, feeling all this to be wrong, could not help making an effort to prevent it. "You will hurt yourself, Miss Bertram," she cried, "you will certainly hurt yourself against those spikes — you will tear your gown — you will be in danger of slipping into the ha-ha. You had better not go."
>
> Her cousin was safe on the other side while these words were spoken, and, smiling with all the good-humour of success, she said, "Thank you, my dear Fanny, but I and my gown are alive and well, and so good-bye."

his plantations in Antigua – so in his absence the family becomes headless. Their straying is brilliantly captured in the episode of the Mansfield family's visit to Sotherton, the great house Maria will command if she marries Mr Rushworth. By now everyone is unhappily in love, Maria and Julia with the theatrical but ultimately indifferent Henry Crawford, Edmund and Mary Crawford inappropriately with each other. The visit takes on symbolic significance, something like Shakespeare's *Midsummer Night's Dream*, as the desiring young people wander off, losing sense of real time and place.

The visit is ostensibly to help Rushworth "improve" his ancient estate. There have already been dubious changes in the house: the chapel is no longer used for public worship.

The place provokes characters to reveal themselves. Henry's flirtatious remark about not wanting to see Maria so close to the altar gives her hope of his affection while suggesting the emptiness of what she is about to undertake. Mary, the sophisticated metropolitan, is appalled to learn that Edmund is to become a country parson. Fanny alone is sad, believing a chapel to be the heart of a house – but her principled views are also aimed at attracting Edmund, now clearly in thrall to Mary's "lively mind".

After this tension, the party goes outside for "air and liberty". They intend to see how an ancient estate might be harmonized with modern vision, but instead they follow desires beyond boundaries that are both physical and symbolic. The future clergyman abandons Fanny, now standing for his duty and rational interest, to follow Mary, who stands closer to sexual desire and licence. Meanwhile, Maria and Henry, facing a locked gate that only Rushworth can and should open, stray into a dangerous place beyond. Maria knows very well the significance of what she is doing. As she remarks, the iron gate and ha-ha "give me a feeling of restraint and hardship".

When Mary Crawford arrived at Mansfield, she believed the London saying that "every thing is to be got with money". *Mansfield Park* gives the lie to this materialism. But to hold the principles enthrined in Mansfield Park is neither easy nor always pleasurable – nor indeed clearly endorsed by the book as a whole. In the end a kind of rigid country integrity wins out – at a considerable cost. There will be silence about so much that is never quite addressed and cannot be if the social order is to remain firm: it is an uncomfortable message in a work that ends with exclusions rather than Austen's usual inclusiveness. In this masterful book the message is delivered with the subtle, sometimes bitter, irony that is Austen's forte.

16

Emma

The heroine of *Emma* is an "imaginist". She inhabits a book of puzzles, conundrums, games, charades and fantasies. Jane Austen herself loved verbal puzzles, and of all her novels this one is the most playful, the most demanding of interpretation – in some ways the most stylishly mysterious. The *British Critic* ignored its mystery but nonetheless turned to it with relief as it did "not dabble in religion".

The heroine has the "lively mind" of Mary Crawford and uses it to create imaginary scenarios. Along with playful words, things too may have different meanings: Mr Elton's court plaster and pencil stub, strawberries, arrowroot and apples, consumer goods from nearby London, the piano, picture frame and folding screen.

At the centre there's a real game, revealed at the end of the novel when the straightforward characters are heartily sick of furtive dealings: only then do they – and we – learn who sent the expensive piano to the impoverished Bates household for Jane Fairfax to play, why Frank Churchill went to London for a haircut, and why Jane insisted on fetching her own letters. Emma's response to understanding this real-life game is extreme: it was "a system of hypocrisy and deceit – espionage, and treachery".

But her own errors and games are only a little less destructive. Trying to make a match for her new friend Harriet, she guesses Mr Elton's riddle correctly but is hopelessly wrong about its purpose. On the Box Hill outing, unknown to Emma, the outsider Frank Churchill is playing his double game by flirting with her, so upsetting his fiancée. Sensing undercurrents, the upright Mr Knightley is annoyed at the riddling centred on Emma – "What two letters of the alphabet are there, that express perfection?" (the response is M A): "*Perfection* should not have come quite so soon," he snaps. Worse follows in the next game when the garrulous Miss Bates declares she will say "three things very dull indeed"; Emma lacks the self-control to avoid responding, "Pardon me – but you will be limited as to number – only three at once." Learning (or failing to learn) not to say what one thinks is a lesson in every one of Austen's novels. In a community the surface must be preserved. It is also important to listen: Emma is mistaken when she declares, "You will get nothing to the purpose from Miss Bates." In fact much can be gleaned from her excited monologues.

In fact Miss Bates is especially necessary to Highbury, both through her kindliness and good will and through her central position. She hears and passes on news and receives much of the gifted food circulating around the village: the pork from Hartfield, the apples from Donwell, baked in the Wallises' oven. And, although she thoroughly irritates Emma, she's actually the most successful "imaginist" with ordinary life: she makes a provincial assembly into "fairy-land" and an unequal society into community by her acceptance of her own status and that of all around her.

Much damage might have been done through game-playing, but in the end what would have been an evil or a gross error in a harsher book such as *Mansfield Park* becomes a "blunder" here. Emma's meddling with the life of the unprotected Harriet could have ended in a broken-hearted girl without prospects, but – perhaps because the Knightley brothers also plot – it instead becomes a comedy of errors. No one has to be cast out, like Maria Bertram, for the kind of scandalous love Emma naughtily and incorrectly imagines for Jane Fairfax.

Austen described Emma Woodhouse as a heroine "no-one but myself will much like", but by presenting so much from her point of view, and by showing her care for her weak father, the author moderates the arrogance and unkindness, making it more comic than threatening. In the carriage ride when Mr Elton proposes to Emma the snobbishness of both emerges: Emma is appalled that he should have thought himself worthy of her, and the vicar that he should have been thought to merit an illegitimate girl like Harriet. He then marries a woman whose ghastliness is seen mainly through Emma's eyes and whose social encroaching she will never control.

Like Elizabeth Bennet, Emma has to learn that she's been socially and intellectually wrongheaded. She's believed that her social position in the village of Highbury – from which she's barely moved in her short life – means she can give status to whomever she chooses: "What! think a farmer, (and with all his sense and all his merit Mr. Martin is nothing more,) a good match for my intimate friend!" she exclaims to the exasperated Mr Knightley. She also knows little of her own needs, putting others forward for the marriage she much later realizes she herself wants – though what she clearly wants is not the marriage to a dashing outsider (which Marianne had yearned for) but the familial marriage that Elinor and Fanny also achieve – and which seems a little disconcerting for modern readers with its whiff of incest and hothouse closeness.

At the start she believes that her control of her present family household is enough:

I am sure I should be a fool to change such a situation as mine. Fortune I do not want; employment I do not want; consequence I do not want: I believe few married women are half as much mistress of their husband's house, as I am of Hartfield; and never, never could I expect to be so truly beloved and important; so always first and always right in any man's eyes as I am in my father's.

The schoolgirl Harriet may be a simpleton but she can see through this, declaring that Emma would then remain a spinster like the (by Emma) despised Miss Bates. Emma is right to say that a spinster with wealth is *not* despised, but life with an ailing, infantile father is clearly unfulfilling. And there's something fearful in her repeated need to marry off others rather than herself, as if she were afraid that her lively, dominant personality could never appeal to anyone she respected. "I know that such a girl as Harriet is exactly what every man delights in – what at once bewitches his senses and satisfies his judgment," she tells Mr Knightley, forgetting, or perhaps refusing to see, that in many cases a large portion is even more bewitching and satisfying.

If Austen thought readers would not "like" Emma, she probably assumed they would approve the man she called Mr Knightley of Donwell Abbey, supposedly her favourite depiction of a traditional rural landowning gentleman – though the resounding name may, as ever, have some irony. He is not perfect. He seems to be as little concerned with the poor of the area as the vicar Mr Elton, though he is good to those in a rank just beneath him like decayed gentlewomen. Uninterested in the aesthetics of estates, Mr Knightley is much concerned with agricultural improvement and the progress of enclosure, which was so changing the landscape and society of England; happily when he considers a path he thinks of the present needs of community as well as his own desires as farmer, though as both major landowner and magistrate he has no need to consult that community. He's open and bluff in contrast to the charming and frenchified Frank Churchill, who is, in Mr Woodhouse's resonant phrase, "not quite the thing". But in the end even the English openness Mr Knightley stands for has its limits. "Seldom, very seldom, does complete truth belong to any human disclosure," remarks the narrator, who keeps Emma silent on her earlier suspicions about the man she will marry – and who refuses to give us what we most want, the romantic scene when Emma accepts the proposal of a man who has, by his own admission, loved her since she was thirteen: "What did she say? – Just what she ought, of course. A lady always does."

17

Emma's First Readers

When George III appeared irrevocably insane in 1811 his son was made Prince Regent, a position he'd long coveted. The Prince was a dissolute figure, much mocked by caricaturists such as James Gillray for his girth, self-indulgence and extravagance.

He formed a striking contrast to his more austere father, who, like Sir Thomas Bertram of Mansfield Park, had failed to instil proper principles in his heir. The Prince had a string of mistresses and had even contracted a secret illegal marriage with Maria Fitzherbert before making a disastrous legal one to Caroline of Brunswick. The ensuing quarrel over custody of their daughter Charlotte led to much very dirty linen being publicly washed.

The Prince Regent was not a figure to command much respect from Jane Austen, who wrote of the royal quarrel,

"I shall support [Caroline] as long as I can, because she *is* a Woman, & because I hate her Husband." So there's some irony in what happened when she visited London to talk to Murray about the publishing of *Emma*.

She was staying in Hans Place with her brother Henry, a widower since Eliza's death in 1813. Here she met a society doctor, through whom the Regent was alerted to the fact that Jane Austen was in London. Apparently he admired her work and had copies of her novels in both his residences; he therefore ordered his librarian, James Stanier Clarke, to invite her to view the Carlton House library. The visit to the hugely ornate house occurred in November 1815. Afterwards Austen felt something was expected of her; so, despite her distaste for his style of life, she dedicated *Emma* to the Prince Regent.

In Clarke himself there was something of Mr Collins from *Pride and Prejudice*; both were courtiers through and through. Once Clarke was the butt of a cruel practical joke: he was made horribly drunk, then put to bed with a donkey. A print, "The Divine and the Donkey", commemorated the event. Austen may have had such an episode in mind when she wrote, "The service of a Court can be hardly too well paid, for immense must be the sacrifice of Time & Feeling required by it."

Clarke, a writer on history and maritime matters, enjoyed meeting Austen and, in the ensuing correspondence, he felt the need to supply her with fictional plots. She might like to write about a clergyman – like himself? Tactfully, she replied that she was insufficiently learned. Since Princess Charlotte was about to marry the German Prince Leopold,

Clarke then thought she might try writing "any Historical Romance illustrative of the History of the august house of Cobourg". She responded:

I could no more write a Romance than an Epic Poem. – I could not sit seriously down to write a serious Romance under any other motive than to save my Life, & if it were indispensable for me to keep it up & never relax into laughing at myself or other people, I am sure I should be hung before I had finished the first Chapter. – No – I must keep to my own style & go on in my own Way; And though I may never succeed again in that, I am convinced that I should totally fail in any other.

Her writing would continue to be "pictures of domestic Life in Country Villages".

Other readers too seemed unaware of what she was trying to do in her novels. Even John Murray felt that *Emma* wanted "incident and Romance", and Maria Edgeworth, so praised by Austen in *Northanger Abbey*, said she read only Volume I, complaining that "there was no story in it, except that Miss Emma found that the man whom she designed for Harriet's lover was an admirer of her own – & he was affronted at being refused by Emma & Harriet wore the willow – and *smooth, thin water-gruel* is according to Emma's father's opinion a very good thing & it is very difficult to make a cook understand what you mean by *smooth, thin water-gruel*"!!

Yet it is precisely making the everyday and the potentially boring bearable – ordinary food, the round of commonplace conversations and encounters – even enjoyable, that is central to the book – as in the passage where Emma, standing at the door of Ford's waiting for Harriet to finish shopping, simply looks at everything:

> *Mr. Perry walking hastily by, Mr. William Cox letting himself in at the office-door, Mr. Cole's carriage horses returning from exercise, or a stray letter-boy on an obstinate mule, were the liveliest objects she could presume to expect; and when her eyes fell only on the butcher with his tray, a tidy old woman travelling homewards from shop with her full basket, two curs quarrelling over a dirty bone, and a string of dawdling children round the baker's little bow-window eyeing the gingerbread, she knew she had no reason to complain, and was amused enough; quite enough still to stand at the door. A mind lively and at ease, can do with seeing nothing, and can see nothing that does not answer.*

A few did understand more fully the power of *Emma* with its complex characters and portrayal of a full and shiftingly layered society. Wanting to help along the sales of his new author, Murray asked one of his more celebrated writers, Walter Scott, to review the novel for the *Quarterly Review*. Scott argued that *Emma* was an example of a quite new sort of writing that had no truck with the sensational and melodramatic; it aimed at verisimilitude, at displaying what was likely, both in actions and emotions. In this new genre, he wrote, Jane Austen "stands almost alone".

WALTER SCOTT ON *EMMA*

"We […] bestow no mean compliment upon the author of *Emma* when we say that, keeping close to common incidents, and to such characters as occupy the ordinary walks of life, she has produced sketches of such spirit and originality, that we never miss the excitation which depends upon a narrative of uncommon events, arising from the consideration of minds, manners, and sentiments, greatly above our own. In this class she stands almost alone; for the scenes of Miss Edgeworth are laid in higher life, varied by more romantic incident, and by her remarkable power of embodying and illustrating national character. But the author of *Emma* confines herself chiefly to the middling classes of society; her most distinguished characters do not rise greatly above well-bred country gentlemen and ladies; and those which are sketched with most originality and precision, belong to a class rather below that standard. The narrative of all her novels is composed of such common occurrences as may have fallen under the observation of most folks; and her *dramatis personæ* conduct themselves upon the motives and principles which the readers may recognize as ruling their own and that of most of their acquaintances."

From an unsigned review in the *Quarterly Review*, October, 1815.

JANE AUSTEN ON WALTER SCOTT

Scott's highly successful novel *Waverley* was published in 1814. Jane Austen recognized that Scott had become the dominant fiction writer in Britain, and on 28 September that year she wrote to her niece Anna:

"Walter Scott has no business to write novels, especially good ones. — It is not fair. — He has Fame & Profit enough as a Poet, and should not be taking the bread out of other people's mouths. — I do not like him, & do not mean to like *Waverley* if I can help it — but fear I must."

EXTRACT FROM *EMMA*

A visit to Donwell Abbey: Emma and Mrs Elton.

It was so long since Emma had been at the Abbey, that as soon as she was satisfied of her father's comfort, she was glad to leave him, and look around her; eager to refresh and correct her memory with more particular observation, more exact understanding of a house and grounds which must ever be so interesting to her and all her family.

She felt all the honest pride and complacency which her alliance with the present and future proprietor could fairly warrant, as she viewed the respectable size and style of the building, its suitable, becoming, characteristic situation, low and sheltered — its ample gardens stretching down to meadows washed by a stream, of which the Abbey, with all the old neglect of prospect, had scarcely a sight — and its abundance of timber in rows and avenues, which neither fashion nor extravagance had rooted up. — The house was larger than Hartfield, and totally unlike it, covering a good deal of ground, rambling and irregular, with many comfortable and one or two handsome rooms. — It was just what it ought to be, and it looked what it was — and Emma felt an increasing respect for it, as the residence of a family of such true gentility, untainted in blood and understanding. — Some faults of temper John

Knightley had; but Isabella had connected herself unexceptionably. She had given them neither men, nor names, nor places, that could raise a blush. These were pleasant feelings, and she walked about and indulged them till it was necessary to do as the others did, and collect round the strawberry beds. — The whole party were assembled, excepting Frank Churchill, who was expected every moment from Richmond; and Mrs. Elton, in all her apparatus of happiness, her large bonnet and her basket, was very ready to lead the way in gathering, accepting, or talking — strawberries, and only strawberries, could now be thought or spoken of. — "The best fruit in England — every body's favourite—always wholesome. — These the finest beds and finest sorts. — Delightful to gather for one's self — the only way of really enjoying them. Morning decidedly the best time — never tired — every sort good — hautboy infinitely superior — no comparison — the others hardly eatable — hautboys very scarce — Chili preferred — white wood finest flavour of all — price of strawberries in London — abundance about Bristol — Maple Grove — cultivation — beds when to be renewed — gardeners thinking exactly different —

no general rule — gardeners never to be put out of
their way — delicious fruit — only too rich to be
eaten much of — inferior to cherries — currants more
refreshing — only objection to gathering strawberries
the stooping — glaring sun — tired to death — could
bear it no longer — must go and sit in the shade."

18

Persuasion

Of the six novels *Persuasion* is the most embedded in national history. Austen began it in August 1815, just when Napoleon was exiled to St Helena, but its events occur in the previous year, 1814, during the false peace, when Napoleon, defeated and sent to Elba, was about to return to France to lead the country into renewed war. The English patriotism of *Emma*, with its love of the English countryside, is here replaced by a patriotism vested in individuals and service. Austen finished the draft in the following year, by which time the first enthusiasm for peace and what it would bring had dwindled.

Henry, who'd done well with his bank and army agency during wartime, went bankrupt; his uncle James Leigh-Perrot lost in the crash, as did the Austen brothers. As a result, Henry and Francis could no longer afford the annual £50 each that they'd contributed to the upkeep of their mother and sisters. The women must have felt their insecurity.

Where *Emma* emphasized place and traditional values, *Persuasion* is about shifting locations and people in process. Its handsome hero Captain Wentworth is no clergyman or landowner but a military adventurer needing to advance his career and make money. In *Mansfield Park* Edmund calls the navy a "noble profession"; Mary Crawford declares it is "well […] if it makes the fortune". Wentworth exemplifies both descriptions. The novel ends, unusually, with the heroine marrying down: to a moderately prosperous captain who cannot settle her on an inherited estate or even in any particular village community but rather promises rented homes and a changing society of professional men. Anne "gloried in being a sailor's wife", helping "the Navy […] who have done so much for us". The great wars are finishing; the novel perhaps asks who deserves to benefit from the peace.

Yet, like Elizabeth Bennet and Emma, Anne herself does value what the inherited estate represents. This is no radical work, though it may be rather idealistic. Anne has become ashamed of her feckless, vain father, forever reading his book of the Baronetage, surrounded by mirrors, failing to manage his property and so needing to retire to Bath: possibly a satiric swipe at the extravagant Prince Regent, who similarly retired from Carlton House to a resort to control his debts. For Anne it's less the house than the responsibilities of the landed class that matter, and if, unlike Mr Knightley in *Emma*, the owner doesn't fulfil them, then he doesn't deserve his authority. As Sir Walter and eldest daughter leave Kellynch Hall to be rented by a sensible naval man who has had the "luck" of war, Anne bitterly observes that "they were gone who deserved not to stay, and that Kellynch Hall had passed into better

NAVAL MEN:
CHARLES AND FRANCIS AUSTEN

Jane's sailor brothers Charles and Francis played a large part in her life, and she pays tribute to them with *Persuasion*. During the twenty-two years of war they served for long periods at sea, while also finding time to marry and produce families. Jane followed their activities minutely and learnt when they fought or captured vessels. (For example, Frank, commanding the *Peterel* in April 1799, captured a fishing boat in the Mediterranean carrying enemy officers and $9,000 in specie: his share of prize money from this one capture was $750.) The brothers were very different. Jane recalled Francis' "saucy words & fiery ways" as a child and his later "warmth, nay insolence of spirit"; he became a harsh disciplinarian. Charles was more popular with his men; Jane described him as "dear Charles all affectionate, placid, quiet, chearful good humour".

hands than its owners". England was fighting France for a conservative vision within Europe, and sailors were interested in their own gain through the war; yet such facts do not affect the idealism vested in men who represent not only martial courage but also "domestic virtues", self-reliance and patriotism.

Part of this idealizing is within Anne's consciousness. Having thought of the navy and its actions for eight lonely years of longing, she makes a sort of halo round all the sailors. Yet they can in peacetime be ill-judging and unsubtle. Wentworth has compromised young Louisa without even thinking of it and is nearly bumped into the wrong marriage for his blindness. Ignorant of his own nature, Captain Benwick thinks his heart broken by one sad reversal, then finds otherwise. And both fighting men are nonplussed by a simple accident on land when Louisa jumps from the Cobb at Lyme. (Indeed, for all their derring-do at sea, naval men seem less endangered than civilians, who contend not only with accidents but also with nervous diseases and debility from inaction and constraints.)

The society to which the naval officers return is not entirely destabilized by their presence. Captain Wentworth will help the admirable Mrs Smith to become a property owner again, while she herself declares she could not have known Mr Elliot's ill-bred wife. And Lady Russell, who reads widely in current affairs, remains impressed with hereditary rank. Both Anne and she despise the obsequious Mrs Clay for her class as well as for her manner. As a result, neither notices her intriguing with Mr Elliot. Anne's younger sister Mary fusses indecorously about precedence over her mother-in-law; in Bath, now past its prime as a spa, Sir Walter and his eldest daughter keep up status by employing unnecessary servants and theatrically displaying a few splendid rooms. And yet Sir Walter continues to *own* Kellynch, and it will go to his unprincipled heir, Mr Elliot, on his death.

If class as a category is gently shaken, so is gender. Anne has to observe her father losing their joint home. And even Wentworth is not so far from the superficial Sir Walter when, on returning, he judges Anne simply by her looks. He demands that women do more than he could ask of any man: that they combine "sweet" femininity with masculine steadfastness, all within the confines of a home. His sister, as "intelligent and keen as any of the officers", should have taught him differently: Mrs Croft has sailed with the husband she deftly controls on land. And there's Nurse Rooke, who, low down the social scale, has practical abilities that would fit her for higher professional status. Anne remains a picture of domestic, not public, authority, her role being as wife and supporter. Even at the end of the novel she "naturally fell into all her wonted ways of attention and assistance".

Yet although she keeps her counsel, Anne is more critical of her society and family than any other Austen heroine – and more hungry for love. At twenty-seven, Charlotte Lucas in *Pride and Prejudice* was prepared to accept anyone for a comfortable home. Anne Elliot at the same age rejects her past represented by the great house, once her home, and the family title, and will settle for nothing less than romantic fulfilment.

EXTRACT FROM *PERSUASION*

Description of Anne's spendthrift father and sister preparing to retrench by renting out their ancestral home of Kellynch.

Vanity was the beginning and the end of Sir Walter Elliot's character; vanity of person and of situation. He had been remarkably handsome in his youth; and, at fifty-four, was still a very fine man. Few women could think more of their personal appearance than he did; nor could the valet of any new made lord be more delighted with the place he held in society. He considered the blessing of beauty as inferior only to the blessing of a baronetcy; and the Sir Walter Elliot, who united these gifts, was the constant object of his warmest respect and devotion. [...]

The Kellynch property was good, but not equal to Sir Walter's apprehension of the state required in its possessor. While Lady Elliot lived, there had been method, moderation, and economy, which had just kept him within his income; but with her had died all such right-mindedness, and from that period he had been constantly exceeding it. It had not been possible for him to spend less; he had done nothing but what Sir Walter Elliot was imperiously called on to do; but blameless as he was, he was not only growing dreadfully in debt, but was hearing of it so often, that it became vain to attempt concealing it longer, even partially, from his daughter. He had given her some hints of it the last spring in town; he had gone so far even as to say, "Can we retrench? does it occur to you that there is any one article in which we can retrench?" — and Elizabeth, to do her justice, had, in the first ardour of female alarm, set seriously to think what could be done, and had finally proposed these two branches of economy: to cut off some unnecessary charities, and to refrain from new furnishing the drawing-room; to which expedients she afterwards added the happy thought of their taking no present down to Anne, as had been the usual yearly custom. But these measures, however good in themselves, were insufficient for the real extent of the evil, the whole of which Sir Walter found himself obliged to confess to her soon afterwards. Elizabeth had nothing to propose of deeper efficacy. She felt herself ill-used and unfortunate, as did her father; and they were neither of them able to devise any means of lessening their expenses without compromising their dignity, or relinquishing their comforts in a way not to be borne.

19

A Romantic Novel?

Persuasion is Romantic in the poetic sense, revealing how words, poems, nature and memories haunt a mind. The novel's plan underlines the haunting, for the second volume echoes the first and brings the past of the heroine Anne Elliot to bear always on her present.

For eight years, an ordinary flirtation with Wentworth – "he had nothing to do and she had hardly any body to love" – has come to determine her present existence. In *Persuasion* Austen tries to catch the movement of a woman's thought, to describe how she feels and how the world appears under tumultuous emotions.

When Anne first sees Wentworth after the lapse of time, the scene overwhelms: "a bow, a curtsey passed; she heard his voice – he talked to Mary, said all that was right; said something to the Miss Musgroves, enough to mark an easy footing: the room seemed full, full of persons and voices". Anne frequently blocks out the external world with her inner feelings; she grows dizzy and surroundings blur: "for a few minutes she saw nothing before her. All was confusion." In a cacophony of noises she manages to hear only Wentworth's voice through "the almost ceaseless slam of the door, and ceaseless buzz of persons walking through".

Sometimes her inner life is so demanding that she appears ill – and indeed the early part of the novel presents a convincing picture of depression brought on by a mind colluding with circumstance. The characters all feel time passing: Sir Walter notes Lady Russell's ageing; Anne loses her bloom as she matures from nineteen to twenty-seven – to the despair of Lady Russell, who calculates worth in the marriage market with the precision of John Dashwood looking at Marianne in *Sense and Sensibility*. Where the early books were so precise about money, here age and dates and bodily accidents and infirmities dominate. The seasons come round inexorably, and the Elliots grow older without the desired social change – even Sir Walter, who believes himself immune to ageing. Anne lets one romantic summer impose on the present and grows sickly under the pain – is "wretchedly altered" in Wentworth's cruel words. In 1814 Jane Austen advised her niece Fanny Knight not to marry a man she didn't love, even if it disappointed him; she continued, "it is no creed of mine [...] that such sort of Disappointments kill anybody". Yet in *Persuasion* Anne comes close to being killed emotionally by letting remembered love become burdensome. Hugging it to herself, she grows dead inside, while on the outside fulfilling her family duties. She refuses to dance but simply plays for others, and she serves her selfish relations while remaining unserved and solitary. She has consciously given in to melancholia. Frequently she withdraws to collect herself and she uses poetry to try to control – sometimes to foster – her mood. Out walking, she quotes to herself the elegiac nature poetry of William Cowper, James Beattie and Charlotte Smith, which stresses human decay and nature's regeneration – although in the bracing air of Lyme she tells Captain Benwick not to indulge in the Romantic poetry of Scott and Byron.

As she serves others and represses herself, she may feel contempt, though she does not openly express it, except by an incipient smile. She inwardly mocks her father and sister for their vanity and snobbery. As she sees Wentworth and the Musgrove girls making mistakes, she "longed for the power of representing to them all what they were about", but she stays silent. Only occasionally does she admire. Her old schoolfriend Mrs Smith is not downcast despite her "cheerless situation", because she lives mainly in the present and doesn't cling to a better past. Anne sees that her friend has "that elasticity of mind, that disposition to be comforted, that power of turning readily from evil to good, and of finding employment which carried her out of herself, which was from Nature alone". She doesn't have this herself – and is not envious.

Anne's intense feelings allow the novel to investigate the closeness of pleasure and pain. Seeing Wentworth in

Bath, she feels confusion, then "agitation, pain, pleasure, a something between delight and misery". Everything is compressed, and she can catch "the happiness of such misery, or the misery of such happiness". Melancholy is diminished by change and bustle, however dreaded, and the body, so often mentioned in this novel, is shaken into greater life, invigorated by wind and weather and new acquaintances. At the end, "when pain is over, the remembrance of it […] becomes a pleasure".

Pleasure is keenest in a rewritten part of *Persuasion* – this novel being the only one for which there are two extant drafts (there is of course nothing conclusive to prove this or any part of *Persuasion* would have been a *final* text). In the first version Anne and Wentworth come together through Admiral Croft. Anne denies what Wentworth had feared, that she was to marry Mr Elliot, and the reunion happens almost wordlessly. On rereading this passage Austen felt the scene "tame and flat, and was desirous of producing something better". She slept on it and next morning "awoke to more cheerful views". The result was a resolution through the scene in the White Hart Inn. Throughout the second volume Anne has been more controlling, seeking out Wentworth, watching for him and intercepting him. Here at the end she probably knows that her talk with Captain Harville is overheard by its subject. When Harville claims the stronger feeling for active men, she argues that claustrophobic female lives breed intensity:

We cannot help ourselves. We live at home, quiet, confined, and our feelings prey upon us [...] All the privilege I claim for my own sex (it is not a very enviable one: you need not covet it) is that of loving longest, when existence or when hope is gone.

The eloquent confession does its work and Wentworth proposes. Instead of accepting a restricted, blighted life (as she implies that she herself had been prepared to embrace), Anne has "all which this world could do for her". It is Austen's most perfect romantic ending.

20

"Sanditon"

From 1816 Jane Austen was ill. She cannot have known she was dying, but she knew her health was poor. It's surprising therefore to find her reverting in her last months to the kind of writing she'd so enjoyed as a teenager, full of parody and caricature – although anyone who reads her letters or occasional poems knows that she always enjoyed absurdity in real life and in fiction. It even begins with an overturned carriage, the old fictional plot device she had exuberantly mocked in her juvenile romp, "Love & Freindship".

Amazingly in the circumstances of her own illness, "Sanditon" mocks invalidism. This last novel fragment exists in three small books, which include three dates: on the first page of book 1, 27 January 1817; on the first page of book 3, 1 March; and the last line of the manuscript is followed by 18 March. Corrections and changes occur throughout, but there are many more in the early pages than in the later ones. Revisions rarely move towards subtlety; instead they often render details more ridiculous and characters more idiosyncratic, as when the energetic busybody Diana Parker says that, to cure a sprained ankle, she's rubbed it without stopping for six hours rather than four. Diana declares she can scarcely crawl from her "Bed to the Sofa" and is "bilious". Poignantly, when Jane Austen thought herself "bilious", she added the term "anti-bilious" to the catalogue of "antis" for which the Sanditon air was to prove useful.

Those who expected her final work to continue the experimentation with psychological realism and depiction of inner life which had characterized *Emma* and *Persuasion* were disappointed, while her family who first read the work were horrified; for some years they avoided full publication by printing only snippets. Later critics too were shocked by the crudeness, occasionally blaming it on the author's ill health. Yet there's a vibrancy to this novel that's quite enchanting; like its invigorating subject, "Sanditon" exists in "Sunshine & Freshness".

An English commercial seaside resort after the battle of Waterloo is the setting. Austen knew her subject as surely as she knew the southern English village that was her usual scene, for since leaving Bath she'd stayed in Lyme Regis, Sidmouth, Dawlish and Worthing. Earlier in life she'd had her characters mock such places: in the juvenilia, Brighton, the Prince Regent's chosen resort, is one of Lady Lesley's "favourite haunts of Dissipation", while Lydia Bennet in *Pride and Prejudice* imagined the streets "of that gay bathing place covered with officers". Many other writers ridiculed the craze for constructing and visiting seaside towns, which had superseded inland spas such as Bath as the resorts of choice for health and recreation. As Cowper, reputedly Austen's favourite poet, noted, "all impatient of dry land, agree / With one consent to rush into the sea". She had already shown her fascination for such places in her description of Lyme Regis and its eroding cliffs, but the visit in *Persuasion* took place in November when sea-bathing was over and almost all the visitors gone.

Sanditon – the name perhaps implying that it's based on sand – is being built on fashion and sickness through the use of enticing words, exaggerated hopes and "wheel within wheel", to use Diana's expression for networking and gossip. About sickness it's ebullient. The most enthusiastic connoisseurs of health and cures are the hypochondriacs, who grow lyrical about their symptoms and imagine extravagant scenarios of harm and remedy. Many moralists of the time blamed the national obsession with health and the body on too much money and leisure: the culture of sickness expended energy on the self rather than on productive work. In "Sanditon" much effort goes into being sick, into sea bathing which needed machines and attendants, and into taking cures which required the construction of chamber horses and the collection of donkeys' milk.

Like *Persuasion*, which combined praise for the entrepreneurial sailors with an appreciation of the old landscape and ways, "Sanditon", with its vital depiction of a new world of seaside hostelries and shops full of modish consumer items, includes traditional attitudes towards the original village community and the great house. Mr Parker's snug ancestral home in the valley has advantages over the windswept hilltop villa to which he drags his family, while the little town (a "young and rising bathing-place" in Mr Parker's vision) depends on passing trade and has lost its surer basis in fishing and farming. The novel opens with Mr Parker, its main sponsor, being overturned in a carriage on the wrong road in the wrong part of the country and mistaking a rural double tenement for a gentrified cottage. In Sanditon the local landowner is a dominating woman: Lady Denham, the last in a line of too powerful older women, from Mrs Ferrars through Lady Catherine de Burgh, who use their money capriciously to control their dependants.

It's unclear where "Sanditon" was going when Jane Austen stopped writing it. Perhaps the economy of the new town would collapse and speculation be proved misguided; perhaps the gothic plot of the absurdly literary Sir Edward – he believes himself "formed to be a dangerous Man" – and the interesting Clara might have ended in the seduction Sir Edward coveted. But there would have needed to be comic resolution of some sort, and it's hard to imagine the breezy and endearing Parkers coming to much harm.

We are all in good health (&) I have certainly gained strength through the Winter & am not far from being well; and I think I understand my own case now so much better than I did, as to be able by care to keep off any serious return of illness. I am more & more convinced that Bile is at the bottom of all I have suffered, which makes it easy to know how to treat myself. You will be glad to hear thus much of me, I am sure, as I shall in return be very glad to hear that your health has been good lately.

From a letter to Alethea Bigg,
Friday 24 January 1817

21

Death

On 18 July 1817 Jane Austen died, wanting, according to her sister, "nothing but death". "She was the sun of my life," Cassandra told Fanny Knight, "the gilder of every pleasure, the soother of every sorrow, I had not a thought concealed from her, & it is as if I had lost a part of myself."

In her last months Jane Austen also had mental anxieties to contend with. Her uncle James Leigh-Perrot had been expected to leave his sister's family some of his very large fortune. On 28 March 1817 he died and the Austens learnt that he'd left everything to his wife; only when she died would they receive the longed-for legacies. "I am ashamed to say that the shock of my Uncle's Will brought on a relapse […] I am the only one of the Legatees who has been so silly, but a weak Body must excuse weak Nerves," Jane wrote.

And there were other concerns. From 1814 her brother Edward had been involved in a lawsuit that put in question his ownership of the Knight estates in Chawton, including the Austens' cottage; the matter was settled expensively only after Jane's death. Meanwhile, brother Charles, with the war ended, had been sent to capture pirates near Smyrna. In the winter of 1816 his ship struck rocks and was wrecked; he was court-martialled and acquitted, with blame falling on the local pilots, but he didn't receive another command for many years.

Jane Austen abandoned "Sanditon" only when she felt herself very ill. At the end of 1816 she'd written a lively letter to her nephew James-Edward describing her own novels as written on a "little bit [...] of Ivory" with great labour. By then she was already unable to walk the distance of less than two miles to his sister Anna Lefroy's house, although declaring herself "otherwise very well".

By the close of January 1817 she felt she'd improved and could imagine walking to Alton, and in February she was writing delightedly to the "inimitable" Fanny Knight about her "queer little heart". But in mid-March she was less ebullient. She'd had a relapse, but believed she was now "quite equal to walking about & enjoying the Air". She was making plans to ride the donkey.

A week after stopping "Sanditon" in mid-March, she admitted:

> *I certainly have not been well for many weeks, & about a week ago I was very poorly, I have had a*

good deal of fever at times & indifferent nights, but am considerably better now, & recovering my Looks a little, which have been bad enough, black & white & every wrong colour. I must not depend upon being ever very blooming again. Sickness is a dangerous Indulgence at my time of Life.

On 6 April she told her brother Charles she'd "been too unwell the last fortnight to write anything that was not absolutely necessary". Three weeks later she made her will, leaving everything to her sister Cassandra except for two legacies to Henry and his cook.

Through May Jane Austen was confined to bed and the sofa, taking comfort in the fact that her "head was always clear". Towards the end of the month, she declared herself "a very genteel, portable sort of an Invalid", and it was decided she should travel with Cassandra to Winchester to be under the care of a surgeon, Mr Lyford. Appreciating the love of her close relatives, she wrote, "if I live to be an old Woman, I must expect to wish I had died now, blessed in the tenderness of such a Family". Repeatedly declaring to correspondents that she was improving, she continued to deteriorate.

Yet on 15 July she wrote one of the light comic poems she'd enjoyed composing throughout her life. This concerned the races that took place in Winchester every summer. It was her last composition – not in her hand for she could no longer hold a pen, but probably dictated. "When Winchester races first took their beginning" played on the popular superstition that if it rained on St Swithin's

Day rain would continue for forty days. It contains the resonant lines with which the saint, patron of Winchester, addresses the neglectful town: "When once we are buried you think we are dead / But behold me Immortal".

On 18 July 1817 Jane Austen died, wanting, according to her sister, "nothing but death". She was buried in the north aisle of the nave of Winchester cathedral. The long epitaph possibly composed by one or more of her brothers does not mention her authorship but, in the Biographical Notice which Henry contributed at the end of the year to the posthumous first edition of *Persuasion* and *Northanger Abbey*, he formally identified his sister as the author of the six completed novels.

22

The Cult of Austen

As Sarah Ball wrote in *Newsweek* 2010: "In the economic doldrums, it is the eminently bankable Austen's blessing and curse to be constantly applied and misapplied. Jane-anything sells out." Jane Austen has entered the global market and culture.

Beyond Walter Scott's famous review of *Emma* little important comment on Jane Austen was printed in her lifetime. She was known and admired by some discerning people but was not a popular author. The decade following her death formed the lowest period in her fame. In 1817, the publisher Egerton remaindered the third edition of *Pride and Prejudice*; thereafter, one by one, her other novels fell out of print.

Only in the 1830s, when Richard Bentley acquired rights to all the novels, did they return to the marketplace, and even then they sold modestly. Jane Austen was admired by distinguished men of letters such as George Henry Lewes and Thomas Babington Macaulay but was considered lightweight beside the serious George Eliot.

Her stock rose towards the end of the century, aided in 1870 by James Edward Austen Leigh's publication of a *Memoir* of his aunt depicting her as a ladylike Christian spinster. England was by now an industrial country crisscrossed by railways: Jane Austen's novels seemed to deliver a lost, genteel, simpler place. Soon the author herself became a sort of national treasure, with gentlemanly "Janeites" growing sentimental over the heroines, especially Elizabeth Bennet. Later still, the novels provided an escape from the horrors of the First World War; Rudyard Kipling's short story "The Janeites" portrays a common soldier joining officers in a secret society of Austen lovers.

"Austenolatry" irritated American writers such as Mark Twain, who wanted to dig Jane Austen up "and beat her over the skull with her own shin-bone!" Equally indignant at the cultish aspect of the admiration were twentieth-century literary critics who found her work less gentle than dark and less escapist than serious. For F. R. Leavis she became the mother of the Great Tradition of moral English fiction. For activist women of both First and Second Wave feminism, the novels were less easily assimilated than her professional image: Austen became useful as a role-model for the struggling woman author who had to use subterfuge to get her message across.

With the arrival of film, the novels took on a new life, appealing to a mass audience which may or may not have read the printed books. Here *Pride and Prejudice* dominated; stripped of most of its irony and delivered mainly as a Cinderella story, it lent itself brilliantly to romantic adaptation. In the 1940 film Elizabeth and Darcy were played by the current heart-throbs, Greer Garson and Laurence Olivier. In 1949 the American NBC also adapted it, while the BBC made four mini-series – in 1952, 1958, 1967 and 1980 – before arriving at the iconic version in 1995, Andrew Davies' six-parter using Colin Firth as Darcy; the added scene where Firth jumps into a lake and emerges with wet clinging shirt and breeches has been watched by millions on DVD and YouTube. In 2004 came a Bollywood version, Gurinder Chadha's 2004 *Bride and Prejudice*.

Although none of the other novels achieved as much cinematic fame, *Emma* has inspired many adaptations, including the Hollywood updating *Clueless* (1995), the Indian *Aisha* (2010) and at least eight television and film versions; and *Sense and Sensibility* gained exposure with Ang Lee's and Emma Thompson's 1995 film. Meanwhile, dramatizations and musicals proliferated from the 1920s onwards, including A. A. Milne's *Miss Elizabeth Bennet* in 1936. A longing for the Austen world inspired television's *Lost in Austen* (2009), where a young contemporary London banker enters the more desirably elegant life of Elizabeth Bennet.

Textual adaptations and continuations started early, with the Austen family exploiting the unfinished "The Watsons" and "Sanditon". Much later, characters in the finished texts left their narratives and gained fuller lives in prequels and sequels. Often they acquired extra, sometimes American, relatives or mingled with society from other novels: James Morland from *Northanger Abbey* meets Kitty Bennet from *Pride and Prejudice*. Fantastic, exotic and erotic scenes were added to the original works, with *Pride and Prejudice* again bearing the brunt since authors could assume reader familiarity with the original characters. (If readers didn't know the plot, they could read Joan Klingel Ray's 2006 primer *Jane Austen for Dummies*). Among other reincarnations, Darcy became a vampire, a werewolf and a sexy rock star.

A few novel bestsellers emerged from this frenzy of exploitation, including Helen Fielding's *Bridget Jones's Diary* (1996), the film of the book referring both to Austen – Bridget's true love is called Mark Darcy – and to earlier film versions; Seth Grahame-Smith's *Pride and Prejudice and Zombies* (2009), the blurb of which declares that the work "transforms a masterpiece of world literature into something you'd actually want to read"; and P. D. James's *Death Comes to Pemberley* (2011), where a drunken Wickham is accused of murdering his friend Captain Denny.

Jane Austen herself has been used and abused for contemporary self-help, and her novels plundered for advice on living, good manners and finding a mate: *The Jane Austen Companion to Life* (2010), *Jane Austen's Guide to Dating* (2005), or *Dating Mr Darcy: The Smart Girl's Guide to Sensible Romance* (2005). Examples of her wit or pithy lines of supposed wisdom have been lifted from the books and stamped on tea towels, pens and coffee mugs.

Meanwhile the novels exist as "chick lit", repackaged in pink and silver; as suitable teaching texts for young people; as counting manuals for toddlers; and in numerous comic versions. They are favourites of the book club, itself the subject of Karen Joy Fowler's *The Jane Austen Book Club* (2004), and have been translated into more than thirty languages. On the internet Jane Austen is served by numerous sites and blogs, including the Republic of Pemberley, and she is the subject of dedicated magazines such as *Jane Austen's Regency World*, published by the Jane Austen Centre in Bath. Appreciation societies proliferate, the largest being the Jane Austen Society of North America (JASNA) with 3,000 devoted members.

Truly Jane Austen and her novels can be customized and delivered in whatever guise the consumer desires. As Sarah Ball wrote in *Newsweek* in 2010: "In the economic doldrums, it is the eminently bankable Austen's blessing and curse to be constantly applied and misapplied. Jane-anything sells out." Jane Austen has entered the global market and culture.

FURTHER READING

Butler, Marilyn, *Jane Austen and the War of Ideas*, 1975;
Oxford University Press, 1987

Byrne, Paula, *The Real Jane Austen: A Life in Small Things*,
HarperCollins, 2013

Duckworth, Alistair M., *The Improvement of the Estate:
A Study of Jane Austen's Novels*, 1972; Baltimore: Johns
Hopkins University Press, 1994

Hardy, Barbara, *A Reading of Jane Austen*, Peter Owen,
1975; Athlone Press, 2000

Jane Austen in Context, ed. Janet Todd, Cambridge:
Cambridge University Press, 2005

Jenkyns, Richard, *A Fine Brush on Ivory: An Appreciation of
Jane Austen*, Oxford: Oxford University Press, 2004

Kelly, Helena, *Jane Austen: The Secret Radical*, London: Icon, 2016

Lane, Maggie, *Jane Austen's World: The Life and Times of England's Most Popular Author*, Carlton Books, 2013

Le Faye, Deirdre, *Jane Austen: A Family Record*, 1989; Cambridge University Press, 1994

Mullen, John, *What Matters in Jane Austen*, London: Bloomsbury, 2012

Tanner, Tony, *Jane Austen*, Houndmills: Macmillan, 1986

Todd, Janet, *Cambridge Introduction to Jane Austen*, 2006; Cambridge University Press, 2015

Wiltshire, John, *Jane Austen and the Body: "The Picture of Health"*, Cambridge: Cambridge University Press, 1992

OTHER TITLES IN THIS SERIES INCLUDE:

The Shakespeare Treasury
A collection of fascinating insights into
the plays, the performances and the
man behind them
Catherine M. S. Alexander
ISBN: 978-0-233-00496-9

The London Treasury
A collection of cultural and historical
insights into a great city
Lucinda Hawksley
ISBN: 978-0-233-00482-2

The Victorian Treasury
A collection of fascinating facts and
insights about the Victorian Era
Lucinda Hawksley
ISBN: 978-0-233-00477-8

The Tudor Treasury
A collection of fascinating facts and
insights about the Tudor dynasty
Elizabeth Norton
ISBN: 978-0-233-00433-4

The Agincourt Companion
A guide to the legendary battle and warfare
in the medieval world
Anne Curry
ISBN: 978-0-233-00471-6

Magna Carta and All That
A guide to the Magna Carta and life in
England in 1215
Rod Green
ISBN: 978-0-233-00464-8